JULIAN

JULIAN
FLEUR
PIERETS

Translated from Flemish by
Elisabeth Khan

3TimesRebel

First published by 3TimesRebel Press in 2023, our second year of existence.

Title: *Julian* by Fleur Pierets

Original title: *Julian*
Copyright © Fleur Pierets, 2019

Originally published by Das Mag

Translation from Flemish: © Elisabeth Khan, 2021

Design and layout: Enric Jardí

Cover photography: © Duncan de Fey

Editing and proof reading: Greg Mulhern, Carme Bou, Bibiana Mas

Maria-Mercè Marçal's poem *Deriva*:
© heiresses of Maria-Mercè Marçal

Translation of Maria-Mercè Marçal's poem *Deriva*:
© Dr Sam Abrams

Author photograph: © Fleur Pierets

Printed and bound by TJ Books, Padstow, Cornwall, England
Paperback ISBN: 978-1-7394528-4-1
eBook ISBN: 978-1-7394528-5-8 / 978-1-7394528-6-5

www.3timesrebel.com

*With my voice,
I am calling you.*

Nick Cave

For Paulien, Julian and Jim — my wife

MY FAVOURITE LOVE STORY IS OUR OWN. IT BEGAN IN Amsterdam on 9 December 2010, and then travelled around the world as an art project. I would symbolically marry my wife in every country where gay marriage was allowed. A performance piece that celebrated those countries that had legalised same-sex marriage and highlight the ones that hadn't. Art broadens the mind, and we wanted to create a greater awareness for equal rights.

When we started in 2017, there were twenty-two countries where two women could marry. And that was the name we gave our project: 22. The name was a conscious decision and we hoped for an extra country to join the ranks while we were travelling. Just imagine, we said to each other, imagine being able to create an exhibition with footage from twenty-three countries. We thought that would be fabulous. During our performance Malta, Germany, and Australia were added to the list. Positive changes were gathering speed worldwide, and our project would become a time capsule documenting it.

The ceremonies were being filmed. A video and photography installation would travel to all the countries we had visited. A book and a 'making-of' documentary were also in the works. Planning for the next five years had been completed. Never before had we looked so far ahead. We were living the life of our dreams.

My wife died on 22 January 2018. We had said 'I do!' in four countries. When she died, all of the light died with her.

AS SOON AS HER BREATHING BECOMES IRREGULAR, I intuitively know that she only has a few more hours left to live. She is lying on her side and I have aligned my body with hers. My hand in her hand, my face against her neck. I can feel the heat of her fever.

I will always love you.
I will never forget you.
You are forever in my heart.
I will never leave you.

Words I have spoken over and over again for the past six weeks, I now whisper in her ear. Now and then I feel myself drifting off and then jerk myself back to consciousness as the pauses between her breaths lengthen. I force myself to stay awake. I have to fight my mind and body's attempts to shield themselves from the reality of what is happening. Outside, day is dawning and I am furious at the sun for shining so effortlessly while my worst nightmare comes true.

Then, the moment comes when I know she will breathe just three more times, then just twice, then just once.

At the New York Met I once saw Damien Hirst's *The Physical Impossibility of Death in the Mind of Someone Living*. He had asked an Australian fisherman to catch a shark that was 'big enough to eat you.' The tiger shark was now suspended in 16500 litres of formaldehyde, and I was shocked to see something so majestic and murderous confined in a show-case made of steel and glass. An ominous creature, with gaping maw, fixing its prey on the other side of the glass. The critics called it a symbol of our own deterioration but, in a flash, what I saw was an animal floating motionless in the water, stripped of any traces of life, yet eerily present. An object soullessly acquiescing to its deathlike shape, subsequently becoming more terrifying than it ever had been.

Julian doesn't exhale. Hopelessness, panic, fear, pain, and the tiger shark all invade my mind as I look at her. Moments ago I was still able to feel her energy but now I'm dreading the absence of that life, the empty shell that had once contained my beautiful wife. A profound love for what is gone and an unreasonable fear of what is still there. I shudder as I gently let go and open a window. I don't know why I'm doing it, but I do know that it's very important. I no longer dare to lie next to her, so I kneel by the bed, put my head on her stomach and cry.

I'm so normal that it almost becomes controversial. Most people still think you have to be a freak to make porn movies.

In conversation with Erika Lust
Et Alors? Magazine

I MET JULIAN AT AN EVENT IN AMSTERDAM. IT FEATURED talks about feminism and gender issues, and the keynote speech was to be given by a porn star. A pregnant porn star, to be precise. She would be discussing her place in a world ruled almost exclusively by men. I'd been nursing a bit of a cold, but I let my curiosity get the better of me. Later, Julian wondered if we might tweak the story somewhat. She thought it sounded a bit lame that we'd met at a lecture about porn. We agreed to say that we had met at a party. Simple. Reality however, had been so overwhelming that I kept forgetting and dragged that porn actress out every time someone asked me to tell the story.

'Sorry!'

'No problem,' she said. 'Next time.'

She, for her part, told people she'd fallen madly in love at first sight. That she was ready to drop everything right there and then. She also said I was wearing a fur coat and a short dress. I've never owned or worn a fur coat in my life, but she remembered that coat in great detail. How reliable are memories? How reliable is everything I am writing down?

The first time I saw her, the light was switched on. In my mind, in my body. Everything came into focus and I knew that she was the one with whom I would do great things.

At the start of the lecture Julian came to sit next to me. After a few minutes she inquired if I, too, thought it was boring.

'Yes,' I said.

I'm not sure whether it was actually true, but in that moment there were too many voices and hers was the only one I wanted to hear. Because I was wondering if she actually existed. If I hadn't made her up. Because she was the most beautiful human being I had ever seen. She was tall, had a buzz cut and an athletic body that seemed to move effortlessly. She was gorgeous. For a split second, my brain short-circuited as I wondered where she'd put herself on the gender spectrum. I wanted to hear what someone like that had to say.

We never stopped talking after that. For seven years, nonstop. There were times when we stumbled over our words because we had so much to say. I had never met anyone who could talk as much as her. And I listened. I interrupted her. Sometimes, we'd wake each other up just to share something. In the morning we then wondered if that wasn't a bit much. But, no. It had been urgent. Necessary. We agreed that would always be acceptable.

That first night she told me about days gone by. About the village in Friesland where she grew up. The first time that she fell in love had been in a sandbox. With a girl. She wanted a home and kids, yet she soon realised that she was not meant to have those things. Even as a child she caught on very fast to the idea that she didn't fit in to that picture. So she kept her mouth shut. Later, she fell in love with a girl in her class and wrote her long anonymous letters. 'Nowadays they'd call it stalking,' she admitted. She was a quiet child, who often sat in her room reading, listening to music or playing the guitar. But, she also had a lot of pent up anger inside her. Until an empathetic teacher encouraged her in running. Fast and long-distance, it made the anger evaporate. On the last day of school she admitted in front of her class to being lesbian. And she confessed to the girl that she had been the one writing the letters. To her surprise, the infatuation had been mutual. So many years, so many letters, so much left unsaid. What a waste of time. What is the impact of all that silence on the rest of one's life?

=

When the undertakers come to collect her that afternoon, they ask me to leave the room. It's the first time in seven years that I'm not by her side. The first time that she won't be in this bed when I return. I have to leave the room because they will be putting her in a bag and that is traumatic, according to the funeral trade's experience.

Everything can always get worse, I think.

With my mother by my side, I hear them at work in the next room. I want to tell them to be careful. That she is so fragile she could break. Your imagination, too, can always get worse. All my muscles are alert, my fingers cramped around each other, my breathing shallow.

Surely this can't be true – the words become a pendulum – *this can't be true this can't be true this can't be true* – until *a clear, but it is!* interrupts my train of thought and everything around me starts spinning. My mother is standing between me and the door. I ask her to step aside. If I don't watch them taking her away, I will never be able to believe it actually happened. It feels as if parts of me have been torn off. Strips of skin that are now being wheeled out of the house in a plastic bag on a gurney.

One of the men approaches me to awkwardly ask if I want to see her again before the cremation. I say yes. I say no. Then yes again. Then no. I think about the sounds in the room and how I couldn't see what they were doing. Seeing her again means they will need to bathe and dress her. They'll have to touch her and I don't know if they will be gentle enough. I'm no longer there to protect her and the thought of that task being in other hands is unbearable.

'No.'

As soon as she's gone, the label of Helpless Woman becomes attached to my identity. It doesn't suit me, and yet that's how I feel. I stare blankly at the wall, walk in and out of the room a few times. She's gone. For six weeks I have been hyper-vigilant. Now there is nothing left.

I'm looking at the pictures I took of her in recent weeks. Sleeping, curled up among the pillows, in the hospital bed, in the living room. She's staring vacantly into space. She's looking at me, slightly out of focus and with a little smile on her face. Photos of our intertwined fingers. Photos of the freckles on her arm. Of that one black mole next to her bellybutton. I can look at her for hours. She is so incredibly beautiful, and her disappearance lends her a translucent, ethereal beauty.

I had been documenting the deterioration, because a picture proved it was happening. That it wasn't a figment of my sick imagination.

'To photograph is to appropriate the thing photographed,' Susan Sontag wrote in *On Photography*. If I photograph her, I will never lose her. If I never lose her, she will always be with me. Strangely enough, that made a lot of sense at that point.

All I can do now is crawl into bed. There is a limit to the amount of reality one can handle. A few hours later I wake up in a panic, thinking about the pictures. If I don't see her again, I'll never believe that she's gone. I call the funeral director, nauseous with anxiety. It's not too late yet. I can still see her. It is now Monday. I'll see her again on Wednesday. I feel butterflies in my stomach, like on a first date. She's not gone yet. I'm going to see her. She's still here.

My movie is based on the desire for transformation and self-determination. I wanted to show that we have much more possibilities than playing a role that is dictated by society.

In conversation with Tim Lienhard
Et Alors? Magazine

I'M TRYING TO RECALL WHO I WAS ON THE DAY I FIRST MET HER.

Confused and loud are two words that come to mind.

I had been married to writer Jeroen Olyslaegers for ten years and the fallout of that breakup was still eating away at me. The end of my marriage had thrown me into a deeper state of emotional distress than I had expected. I thought everything would fall into place once I was single again. I discovered, however, that the lack of freedom had only existed in my head, not in my relationship. It was a harsh lesson. The divorce led to an endless string of transformations and identity shifts, depending on circumstances and short-lived partner choices. I tried blindly to make my way through life, and considered it of the utmost importance that people should like me. My life was an exhausting, downward spiral and, in my pursuit of freedom, I became my own jailer. I partied and drank like a fish. It seemed like a good idea at the time.

'Who are you?' asked the Caterpillar.

'I – I hardly know, sir, just at present,' replied Alice, 'at least I know who I WAS when I got up this morning, but I think I must have been changed several times since then.'

When I first met Julian, I was thirty-seven years old and had moved house forty-two times.

'I can't help it, it's genetic,' I often said. And then I pointed to my mother, my single mother and self-confessed reloca-tion addict. From an early age we moved continuously from one house to the next. The first few months after a relocation, things went well. Everything was exciting and the new house always needed to be decorated. Six months went by, and when I came home from school, the furniture had been moved around. It started off small: pictures on the wall re-placed, a new rug, a vase moved from the table to the dresser. Sometime later, the couch would be where the table had been and the kitchen cabinet would be in the bedroom. My mother would have preferred to sell the lot and replace it with new furniture, but she lacked the money to do so. Once the re-decorating efforts had reached a pace that would be the envy of many an interior decorator, I knew it was time to pack my suitcase again. The pattern made my life manageable. When we walked into a new house that pleased her, she'd look at the kitchen and declare, 'This is where I'm going to cook!' She said it every time, but it never happened. Years later she asked me if she had given me enough to eat. I couldn't re-member ever being hungry, but neither could I remember what we actually ate. I do remember that, in my teens, we sometimes only ate what we liked at the time. Oatmeal and banana, for days on end. Or couscous with canned corn and feta cheese, until we were sick of it. One of her boyfriends once lost 33 pounds after moving in with us for a few months.

Sometimes I dreamed of living in a house that was all mine, and where I could stay indefinitely. I would have chairs and cupboards made out of concrete.

When I was eighteen, I left in order to live by myself. Six months later, I moved the furniture around.

=

Julian's last five weeks were spent at my mother's house in France. The day after her death, I have to go to the funeral home to deal with the paperwork. My mother is coming with me. I haven't been outdoors all this time and the fresh air makes me gag. I walk slowly, stopping every now and then, like an old woman. I realise that Julian will never hold my hand again.

As we enter the funeral home, a shop bell rings, shrill and cheerful. The smell of old carpet hits my nostrils. A row of urns is displayed on the right, plaques and a host of porcelain flower arrangements on the left. Beige, brown, grey. Delicate ceramic petals. I have often wondered how one keeps that clean. So much dust must get in there.

As soon as we sit down, I start crying and can't stop. The man looks at me and takes out his papers. He's seen this many times before. If he has to wait for someone to calm down, then he will never get back to work again. I have to spell her name and, when that won't work, I have to write it down on a piece of paper. My mother takes the shaking pencil from my hand and writes it down. Address. Telephone number.

'Her job?'

'Designer,' I say.

'Comme une créatrice de meubles?'

'Non, comme une artiste.'

'Artiste,' he confirms.

Brutally, he decisively stacks the papers and slams his pencil into the holder with all the others. Then he casually tosses a laminated sheet in front of me on the table. It has an outline of all the coffins they supply. Only the bottom three are suitable for cremation, so my choice is limited. I know I *have* to pay attention now. This is important. But I'm terribly busy trying to control my spine as I keep sliding down the chair.

My mother moves her chair a little closer, so she'll be able to support me should I fall. It stays with me, this tendency to collapse as soon as things get difficult. As if my body decides that it's had enough already.

I point my finger to the darkest coffin. They are all equally ugly. She would hate this.

Later, when I find the strength to read her death certificate, I notice he has written *'sans profession.'* No occupation. Those two words break my heart. Julian considered it so important to stand on her own two feet, to be independent. When she was young she had taken on all kinds of jobs to pay for her studies and earn a living.

'No occupation.' Even in situations like this, inattentiveness is punished.

Androgyny is very difficult to capture in photography because the moment you wonder whether a person is a boy or a girl, that's the moment you see true beauty.

In conversation with Roxanne Bauwens
Et Alors? Magazine

BY THE END OF OUR FIRST ENCOUNTER, I WAS MADLY IN LOVE. She had a playful enthusiasm that made her irresistibly attractive. She smelled of soap and had slender hands and fingers that lay calmly on the table while mine fluttered all over the place.

The day after our first meeting I received a friend request on Facebook from Jim Boh. I didn't know him, but he looked like Julian. With a beard. The info said: Drag king at The House of Hopelezz.

Years earlier I had seen a fascinating exhibition: seductive photos of girls dressed as boys, taken by Risk Hazekamp. Drag kings. One of the pictures shows Hazekamp themself. The word NORMAL is carved into their back with a razor. Another one shows them as James Dean.

Hazekamp says they want to create a reality in which a different identity prevails. The androgynous personality takes centre stage, through archetypal male/female images being united in one person. Later, when we meet Risk in Berlin, there's a statement by gender theorist Judith Butler on the door of their studio: 'The boundaries we draw are invitations to cross them, and crossing them shapes who we are.'

I looked at Jim's photos with the same fascination with which I had looked at Hazekamp's work. How different Jim was from Julian. She was dignified. A melancholic look in her eyes. Somewhat shy. She looked her age — thirty-two, she'd told me. When I met Julian she was wearing All Stars, ripped jeans, and a clean, ironed shirt. Jim, on the other hand, looked like a seventeen-year-old boy with a stubbly beard. He wore a suit and polished black shoes. In some photos he wore only suit trousers and a Guns N' Roses t-shirt. A black hat on his head and cigarette in his mouth. He appeared to be winking at all the girls he met, about to get up to mischief. An impish and confident look. He was gorgeous. She was gorgeous.

The friend request came with a short email: 'Julian told me she likes you.'

What followed was a ten-day exchange between Antwerp and Amsterdam. Between me and Jim, about Julian. Afterwards she told me that she had been so shocked by her own crush that she'd had to cover herself. Hiding behind the tough and fearless Jim seemed like the best alternative. Because, she pondered, could the idea that you had found the love of your life possibly be one-sided?

I asked if she hadn't been able to notice that I felt the same way.

She had. But it had seemed too good to be true.

=

My wife died on Monday 22 January, 2018 at 13 minutes to eleven in the morning. She will be cremated two days later. I'm still in the small village in France where she died. It gives me the excuse to do this all by myself since I am unable to talk to or take comfort from other people. Later, I will feel guilty about this. For not giving her the grand funeral she deserved. But right now, I do what I can and I hate myself for it.

The evening before the cremation I write her a letter. To read to her and to place in her coffin, so that my words will mix with her bones in the fire. In the letter I talk about my gratitude for our wonderful life over the past seven years. For all the love she gave me and that I'd been allowed to give her. All the growth we made together. But, I also talk about my fear. That I don't know how I'm ever going to get over this debilitating grief. How a life without her is not a life, yet I promise I will try.

The sun shines bright on the day of the cremation. I fluctuate between nausea and the apprehension of seeing her again. I'm scared. When the funeral director opens the door to the crematorium, I double over with the pain. He offers to support me, but I push him away and hold myself upright against the wall. I would never have imagined that grief could be so physical.

Once I'm alone I look around. A small room with two chairs. A vase with plastic flowers and a coffin on a wheeled stretcher. Two electric candles flicker at the head end. Together, we would have savoured the old-fashioned kitsch. Without her, it is indescribably sad.

Inside the coffin lies the beautiful shell that was once so full of life. My mother had brought over her black trousers and black turtleneck the day before. Because that was her favourite outfit, and because she was always so cold. I look at her and I don't understand. I don't understand what went wrong and why I'm looking at some thing that resembles my wife, but no longer moves.

Seconds after she died, she was gone. The beautiful body on the bed was empty. My wife had gone. I thought I had imagined it, but now I can see it again. A fundamental 'being' is missing. She still looks like Julian, but she isn't. I haltingly read out my letter to her, with occasional howls and an animal growl in the back of my throat. I put the letter in her coffin and pick up my camera.

=

After Susan Sontag's death in 2004, her partner, photographer Annie Leibovitz, published *A Photographer's Life, 1990-2005*. A collection of over 300 photographs in which everyone recognises her best-known work: a nude and pregnant Demi Moore, Whoopi Goldberg in a bathtub filled with milk, a naked John Lennon clinging to a dressed Yoko Ono. The book was Leibovitz's way of mourning, because 'these photos would never have happened if I hadn't met Susan and fallen in love.'

When they met in 1988, Sontag had said that she was a good photographer, but that she could be even better. Leibovitz, who was at the time looking for direction both in her life and her work, accepted the challenge. 'The notion that she was even remotely interested in my work was very flattering. Even though she criticised it.'

The book also contains many snapshots of the fifteen years the couple spent together. Sontag, playing with her children. At their home. Travelling. Sprawled on the couch together. Naked. During chemo. Sick. On her deathbed. The image of Sontag laid out at the mortuary sparked fierce controversy. The criticism was that Leibovitz could not possibly know whether Sontag had agreed to the publication of the photos, let alone to being photographed. When asked what she thought and felt when she pulled out her camera at that very moment, Leibovitz said in one of her rare interviews, 'I forced myself to take pictures of Susan's last days. I have not analysed that urge. I just knew I *had* to do it.'

=

The funeral director walks in and asks me to leave the room. The coffin must be closed in front of the police and again I am not allowed to witness it. I have trouble breathing, so I step outside. My mother is sitting next to me and I hear her whisper that the sun is shining. From now on my mother says hello every time she sees the sun. She believes it is Julian giving us a sign.

Yesterday I wrote in a post on Facebook that my wife would be cremated at eleven in the morning. I have received more than a thousand responses. From people who would stop for a moment, or light a candle. With all my might, and while I'm staring at the ugly coffin, I try to feel the energy of everyone wishing her a safe journey. Despite the pain, I am grateful that she is being virtually assisted. I had asked the funeral attendants to play George Michael's version of 'The First Time Ever I Saw Your Face.' It always reminded me of her when I heard it. And her of me.

The first time ever I saw your face
I thought the sun rose in your eyes
And the moon and the stars were the gifts you gave
To the dark and endless skies, my love
To the dark and empty skies
The first time ever I kissed your mouth
I felt the earth move in my hands
Like the trembling heart of a captive bird
That was there at my command, my love
That was there at my command
The first time I ever lay with you
And felt you heart so close to mine
And I knew our joy would fill the world
And would last till the end of time, my love
It would last till the end of time

That song is about you. About us, she'd said.

The crematorium can accommodate 150 people and my mother and I are sitting in the front row of an empty room. It's cold, or so I think, and the strange lighting creates a dreamlike haze. Maybe it's my imagination. The slightest movement brings on a huge shift in time and space and, in an attempt to trick the past, present and future, I try to keep as still as possible. Make myself as small as possible. Maybe this will allow me to turn the clock back to seven years ago.

To the moment where I could ask Julian to have a brain scan, even if I had only known her for five minutes.

There is a man standing in the doorway. He looks at us for a while, expectantly, and then walks over. I look at his hands, clasped in front of his chest. He asks if I want to see the coffin heading into the fire. I say no, yes again, then no, and again yes. No one loses patience, and everyone is waiting calmly for me to decide what I want. Or don't want. *Everything could always be worse*, I again think, while the drab curtain slides open at the push of a button. As the coffin moves down the conveyor belt, I think I hear the sound of fire.

*We become architects of our bodies
and designers of our identities. We
merge, we blend, we cross and conjoin
the separations that exist in binary
understandings of gender.*

In conversation with Gabriel Maher
Et Alors? Magazine

IN THE SUMMER OF 2010, SIX MONTHS BEFORE WE FIRST MET,
Julian had discovered her alter ego, Jim. It had started out as
a joke, when a friend challenged her to dress up as a man and
enter a drag king competition. I did not see the show live, but
it's on YouTube. Julian, then still with a painted-on beard (she
would later switch to glueing tiny hairs on her chin), in a white
shirt, a tie and dark sunglasses. She lip-synced to 'Addicted to
Love' by Robert Palmer and was flanked by four drag queens
in little black dresses, with gigantic breasts and squash rackets
for guitars. She won the competition and got to meet the activist and drag queen Jennifer Hopelezz – Richard in real life
– a Greek-Australian doctor who had emigrated to the
Netherlands for love and became the Mother of the Amsterdam
drag troupe The House of Hopelezz. During the monthly
Whores' Ball at Club Church they gathered for lip-syncing
performances, and they stood on the barricades protesting for
equality and diversity during Pride.

Julian loved her two personalities. Jim partied, was dis-
solute, daring, and could do anything without any restraint.

Julian read books, was calm and scientific. 'He assures me I can be nerdy when I want to be, and not worry about being boring.'

The fact that she felt so much freer as a man made her think. She loved performing in drag, but Jim was also a vehicle to show that gender didn't matter. She confused people, and she hoped that this confusion would promote the idea that binary labels are all nonsense. She had always found the man/woman concept strange. Yes, she looked androgynous, and when she shaved her head most people thought she was a man. Nevertheless, she had never felt like she was born in the wrong body. She was a woman, that much was certain. However, she was also convinced that, for the most part, masculine and feminine mannerisms were learned behaviours, influenced by environment, perception, and time.

Forty years ago, it did not occur to people that a woman could be a lawyer, nor was a man expected to spend time with his children. In some cultures it's common for the men to cry more than the women at the death of a child; something that would be considered unmanly elsewhere.

Inspired by a photo series by Jill Peters, I once wrote an article about the Sworn Virgins of Northern Albania. The tradition dates back hundreds of years and is maintained by clans living according to the Kanun. In this tradition, there is an archaic law that designates women as the property of their husbands. Voting, driving, earning money, and drinking alcohol are also the exclusive prerogatives of men. A family that, due to circumstance, is left without a patriarch or male heir, runs the risk of losing everything. Alternatively, young women can assume masculine status (and associated privileges) and become Sworn Virgins or *burrnesha*. To undertake this transition, the women must cut their hair, wear masculine clothing and, in some cases, change their names. Feminine behaviour is unlearned and masculine gestures and 'walks' are rehearsed until they become second nature. After taking the vow of chastity, she becomes a he, and can support their family. The vow of chastity is an important part of this transition, because an unmarried woman must be a virgin. Even when she becomes a man.

When asked whether they would choose the same life path if they could do it all over again, they all said yes. Their status, which has nothing to do with sexual identity or orientation, gives them a kind of freedom they could never have attained as a woman. Even if it's within a community that only grants rights to a woman if she literally wears the trousers. The freedom gained outweighs the restrictions of celibacy.

Encouraged by these theories, Jim/Julian was initially happy when the Dutch television program *Spuiten en Slikken* asked her, together with a number of her peers, to participate in an episode about drag kings. She explained her position on learned masculinity and femininity, but the TV producers edited out the theoretical parts and presented them as a group of lesbians who dressed up as men to pick up women. Julian decided never to participate in that kind of show again. The fact that the heterosexual female TV host wanted to bed her afterwards was small consolation.

=

After the cremation I go to bed, never wanting to wake up again. Auden's words run through my mind.

> *The stars are not wanted now; put out every one*
> *Pack up the moon and dismantle the sun*
> *Pour away the ocean and sweep up the wood*
> *For nothing now can ever come to any good*

I have descended from the highest happiness to the darkest hopelessness. I had foreseen this emotional desperation and, before she died, I had asked her if I could come too. She said no, 'If you die with me, everything we have done will be in vain.'

Nevertheless I've kept her sleeping pills and morphine with me. I need a way out in case I really can't see a future. Twelve sleeping pills and seven morphine patches. I'm mad at myself for not even being sure if it's enough. In his book *On Suicide*, Jean Améry wrote that psychology is inadequate with regards to suicide, because self-chosen death contradicts 'the logic of life.' Camus, too, said: 'There is but one truly serious philosophical problem and that is suicide. Judging whether life is or is not worth living amounts to answering the fundamental question of philosophy.'

Suicide cannot be rationally talked about because everyone in the room seals up as soon as the topic is broached. Eyes grow wide with concern and you are given an unsolicited laundry list of reasons that do make life worthwhile. I don't need to hear the reasons. I know them and have lived them. I just want to know if there is an alternative.

Twelve sleeping pills and seven morphine patches. After a week I throw them in the bin. They make me feel unsettled and I fear I might use them on a whim. And, I've promised her to stay. I've also noticed my mother's worried looks when she brings me food on a tray so I can eat in bed. I can't possibly have her experience what I'm going through right now. She wouldn't survive it. To keep on living for someone else. It's a good enough reason. For now.

I give myself a two-year ultimatum. It's a solid and comforting idea: if I still miss her as much as I do now, still feel so much pain, still see no reason to keep on living, then I can leave. But, then at least I will have tried. It won't be an impulse, but a well-considered decision. A friend once told me about an acquaintance who ordered a Chinese euthanasia kit and used it to end his life in a simple and elegant way. Because sticking your head in the oven or jumping in front of a train is too messy for those left behind. My friend found it reassuring, the idea that this kit existed. I understand what she's saying. Suicide as an alternative, to make life more bearable. Knowing that the possibility exists, at times, suffices for me to quell the panic that the thought of 'time without Julian' evokes. When all else fails, when all possibilities are exhausted, there is always death. What an invention.

I find the same thoughts expressed in the words of Julian Barnes, who also lost his wife to a brain tumour, thirty-seven days after diagnosis. 'I will give it x months, or x years, and then, if I cannot live without her, if my life is reduced to mere passive continuance, I shall become active.'

'All the work we've done will be forgotten,' my wife said when she knew she was going to die. Not in a sentimental way, but matter-of-factly.

'I'll make sure that doesn't happen,' I said, 'I'll write about us.'

'I'd like that,' she said. 'But you don't owe me. Know that.'

Postponing suicide because I'm the only one who can keep her memory alive. I have two years to do so. Big words, while I have no idea if I'll ever get up again.

I try to promote dissident sexualities and am inviting the viewer not to feel ashamed if they want to experience their sexuality in a different way to what is so-called 'normal.'

In conversation with Rurru Mipanochia
Et Alors? Magazine

AT OUR SECOND MEETING, THERE WAS ICE ON THE INSIDE OF the windows of the train from Antwerp to Amsterdam. I shivered uncontrollably in my black dress and she, too, had dressed for a memorable second meeting, rather than for the freezing cold. It took her a few seconds to spot me, and in that brief moment I saw her nerves give way to a shy smile.

'You're not wearing enough clothes. You need to take better care of yourself.' She would repeat the latter part of that phrase for the rest of her life. I don't take care of myself. I never did. I can live on tea and cookies for days, work until I drop, and if I only get two hours of sleep because of a party, then so be it. Once, I spent twenty-four hours hooked up to an iron IV. How did I even manage to get out of bed, the doctor wanted to know? I admitted it hadn't been easy, but I didn't want to be a whiner. During those seven years, circumstances would change, but my propensity to not take care of myself remained.

Julian put me in a taxi and we went to her house, where she made me coffee. After two cups, I had to go out onto the patio to catch my breath. I had been too self-conscious to say I never drank caffeine.

'You need to take better care of yourself.'

She worked as a hydrographer, mapping the seabed. I thought it was very romantic. And, the fact that she had learned to navigate by the stars was amazing.

'I love the sea,' she told me. 'The smell of it, how it looks, both above and below the water. Everything that remains to be discovered, and everything that we are incapable of discovering. Did you know, for example, that we know a hundred thousand times more about the moon than about our own oceans?'

I shook my head.

'I think that's so cool!'

She had grown up by the sea and her father was a sailor. She'd joined the rescue team as soon as she was old enough. Being roused by a bell in the middle of the night, putting on a wetsuit and getting on the boat in all kinds of weather. Sometimes, just to pull drunk tourists out of the receding tide, but more often to provide assistance to ships in need.

It took her a while to decide on her definitive profession. Her creative side wavered between music, literature, and the sea. She studied literature for a year and played in a band, but then made the switch anyway. 'I wanted to learn an old-fashioned trade related to the sea. And, it was either becoming a captain or an engineer. We are a rare species, us hydrographers.'

She travelled the world, sometimes working on drilling platforms, and sailed to India, Africa, wherever land was being expanded and measured.

Julian lived in Amsterdam. I lived in Antwerp. She had a permanent job. I worked as a freelance journalist and wrote articles for newspapers and magazines. Just days after our first meeting we'd already decided we wanted to stay together, so I was spending most of my time in Amsterdam. We had neither the time nor the inclination for the standard getting-to-know-you phase. We wanted to be together, that was the only thing we knew for sure.

'What does a lesbian bring on a second date?'

'A U-Haul.'

This joke was written by lesbian comedian, and *Orange Is the New Black* star, Lea DeLaria. In the wake of her show, the term 'u-hauling' came into use (after the removal van hire company, U-Haul). Some sociologists attribute the behaviour to the homophobic 1950s and 1960s, when gay couples had to keep a low profile. If you were lucky enough to find a partner, you stuck with them. Monogamy was safety. Psychologist and LGBTQ+ activist Lauren Costine endorses this idea, adding that we live in a world which still makes women feel that a relationship is the number-one goal in life. In her book, *Lesbian Love Addiction*, she also suggests a second reason why women start living together so quickly: the production of oxytocin, also known as the cuddle hormone. It plays a vital role in childbirth and in falling in love. It's a biological incentive to bond. The maths is easy: two women, twice as much oxytocin, twice as much desire for connection.

'What does a gay man bring on a second date?'

'What second date?'

=

My days go by in a haze, and all I can think about is that I want her back, that I want to go home. But, she's never coming back and there is no home. When we started our wedding project, we sold our house and all our belongings in order to travel freely.

Each with a suitcase and a lot of enthusiasm. She was my home, and it didn't matter where we lived. But, a decision made with so much love now leaves me in a total void. Two people became one, and the whole world suddenly made sense. How can I ever unlearn that? When one of us is taken away, all the magic and beauty that gave meaning to our lives also disappears.

I sleep with her hat and scarf. The only items of clothing that have retained her smell . I can smell warm caramel, leaves in the rain, and undertones of Tom Ford for Men. Every morning I wake up with a smile, thinking for a second that the world is exactly the way it ought to be.

It always made us laugh when we woke up to find we had been holding hands during the night.

What if all my happiness, all my enthusiasm, all my zest for life, existed only in conjunction with her? What if it's not gravity that holds me in place? Is the sun, sparkling flashes of light in the sea, still as beautiful and amazing when you are the only one looking?

I read about a cult today, and thought about how wonderful it would be to be part of it. Not having to make decisions. Wearing the same clothes every day. Clear definitions of what to believe. I imagined lots of sun and greenery. I would sleep a lot and would then be told to sweep. Wielding a broom in the sun on a veranda every day, no further obligations, no ambitions, no decisions.

Why is love measured in grief? Jeanette Winterson wonders in *Written on the Body*. I measure and map my love for Julian. Now I am the hydrographer.

Who doesn't want to be a lip-syncing, crossdressing lesbian?

In conversation with Landon Cider
Et Alors? Magazine

EVERY DAY I MARVELLED AT HOW DELICIOUS MY WIFE smelled. How easy it was to be with her. On the weekends she showed me around Amsterdam. We walked the streets for hours, had picnics in the parks, and read to each other from the newspaper's culture section. From her bed we watched the hundreds of green parrots that lived in the trees behind her apartment. The story went that someone had released their illegal, exotic pets, and then they had multiplied like crazy. Sometimes, one of them would come and sit on the windowsill. We called her Stella, because I'm a Tennessee Williams fan.

She introduced me to music I had never heard of and made me try food from every country she had visited. I was her date for the wedding of photographer Jan van Breda and his husband Thijs Timmerman, a wedding that was also a celebration of the first same-sex marriage that had taken place ten years earlier, on 1 April 2001, in Amsterdam.

I, in turn, took her to art exhibitions and gave her books by Siri Hustvedt and Jeanette Winterson.

During the week she rode her bicycle to work, where she performed complicated calculations. I didn't understand the first thing about it, but I loved hearing her talk. She took me to parties where men were women and women were men and spent hours in front of the mirror turning Julian into Jim. She shaved her hair and kept the cuttings. Patiently, she'd glue the bits of hair to her jaw with a mixture of oil and foundation. Never mind that it was terribly itchy. The fact that I could only kiss her on her nose and forehead (otherwise I would get covered in hair) was annoying, but made going back from Jim to Julian all the better afterwards.

I watched her from the edge of the bathtub and learned new things. First of all, her breasts needed to become invisible. In earlier times they were tightly bound with cling film or even duct tape, which inevitably caused irritation. Special elastic vests are available today. They look like tank tops and flatten the breasts. Getting them on and off is a chore, but they are not uncomfortable. The outfit also includes boxer shorts and a penis. Available in different sizes. Julian had chosen a medium. 'Let's keep it credible.'

When she was all set, she looked like a sixteen-year-old rascal instead of the tough guy she was always aiming for. I refrained from telling her this.

From an early age I had always wanted to join the circus. I had no particular skills. Because of my fear of heights, the trapeze was out of the question. I was not good with animals, and to this day I have an irrational fear of clowns. Nevertheless, the concept of a nomadic life and the company of fellow wanderers attracted me. Later, I discovered that my fascination was not with circus artists, but with people who lived on the margins. Tod Browning's movie *Freaks* became one of my favourites, and discovering Diane Arbus opened up a whole new world to me. That's how I wanted to spend my life. Her portraits of giants and dwarfs, of the genderless, and of performers, paint a picture of isolation and loneliness, but they also speak of courage and mystique. One of the most beautiful descriptions of Arbus is found in Patrick Roegiers' biography: 'She sometimes looked like a princess who moved haphazardly through her own fairy tale, which was populated by dwarfs, men who are actually women, women who are men, chauvinists, twins, triplets, people in disguise or dressed up, or loaded with jewellery but with no clothes, as if they had suddenly been X-rayed, and all of them determined to show her who they thought they were. And she was the princess on the edge of the fray.'

I was a romantic and Julian's world brought the fairytale one step closer. The Dolly Trolley party at Club Church, her as Tom Cruise in Top Gun. Khaki overalls with emblems and aviator shades. Me with a plastic model plane in my hair and a top made from a Remove Before Flight banner. Stewardesses with beards, pilots in leather suits, and women who became über-women: the faux queens, women who dressed as drag queens.

=

Born in England in 1847, Annie Hindle could be called the world's first drag king.

While there had been actresses before her who had integrated a masculine persona into their acts, Hindle was the first not to create a caricature. The audience saw a cigar-smoking, well-dressed man, and never realised they were looking at a woman. In 1867 she caused a furor in New York, as Charles. Her performances were startling. One of the reviews said, 'Annie Hindle is a great success. Her gender is so perfectly disguised that people think they are watching a man sing.'

Hindle's gender-transgressing behaviour was not limited to the stage, and in June 1886 she married her dresser, Annie Ryan. They were married as husband and wife and the ceremony was performed by a pastor. When questioned about the wedding, he later stated, 'The husband gave me her – I mean his – name. Charles Hindle. He assured me he was a man. The bride was a sensible girl and also an adult. I had no reason to mistrust the matter. I believed they loved each other and would be happy.'

Annie Hindle and Annie Ryan retired to a home in New Jersey where, dressed as women, they were a beloved part of the community. When Ryan died in 1891, Hindle said she'd lost the best thing in her life. The date of Hindle's own death is still disputed, but she lives on in a long succession of drag kings she inspired.

=

Whenever people asked me if I had a happy childhood, I nodded with conviction. I was loved, well cared for and well fed (at least we think so). My mother loved the visual arts. Louise Bourgeois and Picasso were among her favourites. She listened to Maria Callas and Billie Holiday. She taught me one of the most important lessons: 'If you don't know something, look it up. Never settle for ignorance.' Piles of books. First from the library, later from the bookcase at home. Which my mother thoroughly inspected after I'd ferreted out Xaviera Hollander's *The Happy Hooker*, which graced every 1970's bookshelf.

My mother taught me to read when I was four. I could play chess when I was six. No wonder I did so well in school. I didn't have many friends because I liked reading better, and if I played outside on rare occasions, I'd have accidents. Before I turned twelve, I had already broken my arm three times: falling off my bicycle, out of a tree, and off a horse. I'd found the latter at the neighbours' and had been curious if I'd be able to do it, horseback riding. As a result, my mother bought me even more books.

After Julian's death, my mother's advice is still golden. I don't know how to deal with mourning. With that all-consuming grief, and the words *This will never be okay* which, every waking moment, invade my consciousness like a mantra.

The first books I read are self-help books and memoirs by widows. They don't teach me much. There's nothing to read about a lesbian couple. Most widows are older and have had a full life with their partner. Almost all of them have children, and therefore an urgent reason to get out of bed in the morning. Most of these books fill me with rage over their cloying pathos. Yet, they are the only people I want to read about, those widows, those women who have also been through this. They know something others will never know, they're the only ones who can understand the authenticity of this horror. Widows are the only people who can confirm – and feel – that this is murderous. For others it remains guesswork. 'She knows something I'm just discovering,' Joan Didion wrote in *The Year of Magical Thinking*.

I read to get a grip on myself, but we all use the same words of impotence. We all fight with language.

*People change, evolve. I don't exist in the
past tense. It's really bizarre if someone
thinks that I'm not like I used to be. Well
no! Surprise!*

In conversation with Boy George
Et Alors? Magazine

MY COMING OUT WAS THE EASIEST ONE COULD POSSIBLY
imagine. I told my best friend, Renate, that I'd met the most
beautiful creature I had ever seen. Renate Breuer is a writer
and the least judgmental person I know. I'd known her for
twenty years, but we had only recently rediscovered each
other. I was recovering from my divorce, she from a burnout.
Two bruised people, a bar, and a lot of white wine. It was
friendship at first sight. Later, I called my mother in France
to tell her I had fallen in love with a girl. Both of them had
responded with an enthusiastic 'How nice!' My mother is
always a passionate supporter of everything I do, as long as
I am happy, remain polite, and have good table manners. It's
a privileged position. Many people grow up in a homophobic
world, lacking role models. From marketing to films and
advertising, everything is based on the assumption that we
live in a heteronormative world. Anything beyond that is not
normal. In this context, psychologist Lauren Costine refers
to *toxic shame*. The gay child who thinks they are flawed
because they're different from everybody else. One of the

initiatives trying to remedy this is *It Gets Better*, an internet project created by writer and gay activist Dan Savage and his husband Terry Miller. It was founded in 2010, in response to the sky-high suicide rates among gay youths. Since most young people keep their sexual orientation a secret, it's impossible to put an exact figure on the number of suicides among young lesbian, gay, and trans people. However, the Suicide Prevention Resource Center estimates it's four times that of heterosexual youths. Often, the cause is bullying or being disowned by their family. Savage and Miller's goal is to lower those numbers by getting adults to affirm that life gets easier at some point. Meanwhile, more than 60,000 videos have been shared, including by celebrities such as Cher's son Chaz Bono, Lady Gaga, and Ellen DeGeneres. Barack Obama, too, has promised to continue working for a world in which LGBTQ+ youth have a future.

When people asked me if I was lesbian or bisexual, it left me speechless. What strange words, I thought. Are they talking about me? I fell in love with Julian with an open mind, without realising that she was a girl. But, isn't that what love is all about? About falling in love with a person? When I first saw her, I saw the love of my life. Sometimes, things don't have to be so complicated.

=

The first time I was confronted with death, I was five years old. I was lying on my back in the garden, in the morning dew. My great-grandmother came out of the house and asked me to get up, saying I would get sick. I persuaded her to lie down next to me, and pointed out my favourite shapes in the clouds.

A few weeks later she was dead. I always thought it was my fault, and that she'd died of pneumonia. I never talked about it again, and pushed down every thought of her. I never again gazed at the clouds while lying on my back in a garden. Thirty-six years later, I heard my father casually mention that his grandmother had died of a stroke.

Even now, my guilt interferes with any kind of progress. Did I do enough for Julian? Should I have sought a fourth and fifth doctor's opinion? Was I present enough?

If grief is something that grabs and mauls you, then guilt is a toothless beast. A creature that works its way through your belly, through your stomach, and into your heart. There it lies. Pushing and pulling with its big jaws until it almost bites through, but not quite. I'm not even sure if there's a word for this toothless gnawing.

Every night I wake up in a panic. My face wet with tears. I hear faltering breath. It's mine.

Inhale for three seconds. Exhale for eight.

A trick against hyperventilating. Keep breathing. Keep counting.

What if she could still have been saved? There might have been a cure somewhere, and maybe I didn't search hard enough. Did I let her die?

Inhale for three.

I have made hundreds of lists already. A summary of all the symptoms and the reasons why she could never get better. Still. The thought recurs, and I need to list everything once again. My head won't accept my powerlessness. I've failed to save her.

What if she's not happy where she is now? What if she's in pain, what if it's dark out there, what if she's scared? And there's nothing I can do to make it better.

I read somewhere that you can control your emotions by putting an elastic band round your wrist. I snap it whenever I feel my guilt rising. After two days my wrist turns red and blue and there are streaks of blood on the bedsheets.

'Guilt is the gatekeeper of grief,' says Jeroen, when I tell him about my fears that I didn't do enough. He had watched his father die and felt guilty for a year about some small occurrence that any reasonable person would call a minor detail.

My memories come and go, morphing into a scenario where I could have prevented it all.

Changing identity through cross-dressing is somehow a fantasy and has something surreal about it. In order to have the courage to do so, one has to be brave and have a strong personality.

In conversation with Lukas Beyeler
Et Alors? Magazine

INSPIRED BY MY INFATUATION AND BY JULIAN'S FRIENDS, I had started writing about drag queens, queer artists and trans writers. Years later this would become a trend, but at that point I found no buyers for my articles. Only *Elle* published my piece on Julian as a drag king. 'She's a boy, sometimes,' was my headline. Complemented by Jan van Breda's beautiful photos, I wrote about how she would regularly dress as a boy to test both her limits and those of others. More newspapers and magazines followed suit and devoted a whole page to her.

Next, I wrote a long article about Jennifer Hopelezz. About all the family members. About her 'children' Gina and Tina Hopelezz. About the rabbit and the horse, Bunny and Horsy Hopelezz. Her work for the Gay Monument and Pink Point, and her vision on the threshold-lowering combination of drag and politics. The magazines that I submitted the article to responded with a startled, 'This really is too weird.'

'Why don't we start our own magazine?' Julian asked after another rejection. She had no idea how these things worked, but everything could be found on the internet, she reasoned. We'd been together for six months and were about to start our own magazine. We had no idea what to do or how, but if others could do it, so could we. 'And better,' she added.

As Astrid Lindgren's Pippi Longstocking said, 'I have never tried that before, so I think I should definitely be able to do that.' This approach would become the blueprint for the rest of our lives together.

Et Alors? That's what we were going to call it. *'Et alors?'* ('So what?') was French President Mitterrand's response when a journalist from *Paris Match* asked him in 1994 if it was true that he had an illegitimate daughter. His laconic answer became a classic quote and I had always found it amusing. Shameless, too. What better title could we find for a magazine that would cover gender, drag, feminism, and art?

We decided to write and photograph most of it ourselves and we posed for the first cover. If we were going to ask people to reveal themselves, we had to initiate the trend ourselves. What the cover should look like was in my head, as if it had been there, waiting to be photographed, for years. Julian and I, both dressed in white, against a blue background. I wore gloves by Silvia B, a Rotterdam artist who created gloves incorporating so-called beauty flaws. Like a second, imperfect skin. Gloves with birthmarks from which hairs sprouted. Gloves with scars, with LOVE-HATE tattooed on the knuckles. For the photo, I was wearing The Mutant Model, a six-fingered glove. An extra thumb next to my little finger. Julian wore a glued-on beard and an unbuttoned shirt that revealed the mounds of her breasts. The outlandish result was wonderful, and would also give us a unique insight into what people zeroed in on. For example, we received emails telling us we had missed something: we had forgotten to edit out my extra finger. We also received compliments on what a great job we had done adding Julian's breasts in Photoshop. It reminded me of the circus, of the bearded woman who was basically just a man in a dress. Perception is everything.

The first cover of *Et Alors?* was both who we were and who we would become. It was a moment from a time pregnant with the future.

=

I am watching the television interviews we gave about 22 and I'm listening to all the audio recordings I made. Her voice in my headphones. One was recorded in Madrid, where we visited an Indian astrologer. He only had time for one of us. I decided she should go. She had more specific questions about the future: so many ideas, so many plans. What to do first? The astrologer took his time and spoke about her ambition. How important it was for her to be involved. He said she knew what she liked and didn't like. She could use this as a guideline and trust her intuition. About me, he said that I had the ideas, but that she could make them better. *Try to view her as a professional opportunity,* he said. *Follow her, facilitate her, and leave your mark.* Two hours later she left the room in awe. She had recorded the conversation.

I listen to the recording again. Needing to hear her voice, but also looking for clues. Had the man known anything?

Had he said something that we had overlooked? I listen to his description of my wife. As if he, and not I, had been living with her for years. He knows her so well, I think. At the end of the conversation, he presents a timeline.

'Until May 2017, your planets will be under the influence of Venus. This is the best time to position yourself on a professional level. You're looking into creativity, into the arts. In November of the same year you will undergo a major transformation. The beginning of a learning process that will take seven years. There will be a change in your financial circumstances. You will move in 2019. After 2020 ...'

*I feel very lucky to be born a gay person
in a straight-privileged world.
I feel it gives us licence to look differently
at tradition and the way society wants
you to be. It allows us to reinvent
ourselves constantly, because there is no
set path that we have to follow.*

In conversation with Meg Allen
Et Alors? Magazine

BY CREATING *ET ALORS?* WE SATISFIED OUR CURIOSITY. THE magazine became a playground and it mapped out the world we lived in. Fascinated by identity, we wanted to know how queer artists, writers, and musicians had shaped themselves, what they had inherited and what they had bequeathed. Their view of the world. As a woman, as a homosexual, as a trans person.

'If I can't dance, I don't want to be part of your revolution,' said activist and writer Emma Goldman. We treated it as a game to search for a positive tipping point within a given problem. To emphasise everything that is possible. Staying on the sidelines was not an option. We wanted to be in the middle of things. And shout. We wanted to find a common narrative.

We talked to queer artists like photographer Meg Allen, who from 2012 to 2017 photographed all the butch women she encountered because she didn't see herself represented anywhere in mainstream media. We interviewed the Sisters of Perpetual Indulgence, a group of men who have been dressing like nuns since 1980 to educate people about the AIDS epidemic. What started as a small group of activists has now grown into a worldwide organisation.

Writer Jonathan Kemp told us there is a certain kind of courage that comes from having to live outside the mainstream model: 'Few things are more powerful than realising nothing is expected of you.'

Being straight comes with a script. You are aware of the expected trajectory. The model your parents, grandparents, teachers want you to conform to. Like buying a house, having children. Not that every straight couple does this, but when you are born without that script, you are forced to create new possibilities. From that point of view, there is nothing more liberating than not having to live up to expectations.

We were hoping that *Et Alors?* would encourage readers to follow their own path. Especially young people, as far as Julian was concerned. It was a magazine she'd have wanted to read for herself when she was younger. That's why it had to be in English, online, and available for free. As few thresholds as possible. I still remember the look on her face after she read one of the first email responses we received. A fifteen-year-old boy from Texas wrote that he liked to wear dresses but couldn't do so in his community. On the internet he could find only 'extreme cases,' as he put it. In *Et Alors?* he had read about people like himself. About people who used their 'otherness' in their work. He was relieved, and also inspired. Julian wrote him a long e-mail and printed out his letter. With shining eyes, she tacked it to the wall of our office.

'We're doing something right,' she said, lovingly stroking the paper.

Seven years later, *Et Alors?* had grown into an online platform with more than 750,000 readers.

Our roles had been assigned. I searched for the artists and wrote the articles. Julian took charge of the layout and the website; learned to use Photoshop and InDesign. Something she had never done before, but taught herself in no time at all. With admiration I watched her grow into a designer who confidently knew what her ideal magazine should look like. Her love for sleek, stylish, and clear design ensured that even our most inaccessible pieces did not deter the reader. Recognition and style became a means of building bridges.

I remember most of the interviews from start to finish, and there are some that still put a big smile on my face. Such as the conversation with fashion designer Bernhard Willhelm, who talked about how he'd play with perception. For example, he worked with porn stars to present his non-pornographic collection. 'I think that's very exciting,' he said, 'and eventually I get a hard-on. When Bernhard wakes up with a hard-on, it's a very happy day.'

Julian giggled because, apparently, I'd turned beetroot red.

'Teenager!' she teased. I protested vehemently.

Michael Cunningham was our first 'celebrity interviewee.' The writer of, among others, *The Hours* happened to be one of my favourites, and I was definitely being my usual neurotic self while perusing, weeks in advance, every interview that could be found online, rereading all his books, and getting lost in my multitude of notes.

Prepared like never before, I shook his hand. 'I am Fleur and this is my wife Julian.'

There was an ominous silence.

'Did you say, *my wife*?' he asked.

I nodded.

'What a pity. She's the prettiest boy I've ever seen.'

My wife blushed, and he kept gazing at her all through the conversation.

Sometimes we were lucky enough to get to interview our childhood heroes. It was Pride Day in Antwerp and Boy George would be there. From the many interview requests he had picked *Et Alors?*. The Pride's theme that year was 'sports,' and, given our love for fancy dress parties, we were totally in the mood. Julian went as Jim, wearing tennis shorts and a polo shirt. A beard and a tennis racket completed the look. Truth be told, I felt a bit embarrassed shaking my childhood hero's hand in a micro mini tennis skirt, with five shuttlecocks bobby-pinned into my hair. I broke the ice by telling him that as a teen I had been deeply in love with him. That my room was papered with posters and that I'd watched Top of the Pops every week with anticipation, whenever Culture Club released a new single. He looked at me and then at Julian. 'You used to be in love with a man in make-up, now you're married to a woman with a beard. It all works out in the end.' In the hour that followed, we became best friends and I got to ask him all about his alcohol and drug addiction. Something his manager had explicitly forbidden.

=

Two weeks after her death I hear about an event that had taken place at the music club Paradiso, in Amsterdam. They had been projecting pictures of people who had meant a lot to the LGBTQ+ community. Julian's picture was among them. Jennifer/Richard writes there was applause when her picture appeared. Some people were crying.

Jeroen informed me that he had attended a Dez Mona concert where singer Gregory Frateur had dedicated a song to Julian.

Here, in this bed, in this bedroom, alone in France, I had almost forgotten that there are other people who loved her and who have to carry her death with them into their lives.

FROM THE MOMENT I MET JULIAN, I FELL UNDER THE LGBTQA+ umbrella. Lesbian, Gay, Bi-Sexual, Trans, Queer, Asexual. And the +, that too. Because, who knows what else we will come across under that rock? Better to play it safe and take that into account.

I do not like it. I cannot imagine that an L knows what it's like for a T to feel so alienated in their own body that they will undergo the most drastic surgeries in order to find stability. And I'm sure a male T can list hundreds of differences that distinguish them from a female T. And what about that A? 'Asexuality is a term used to describe people who are not sexually active, but it is more appropriate to speak of a lack of sexual attraction,' the definition reads. In other words, this is about people who have no interest in sex. Now, I ask you, what does that have to do with two men or two women who are in love with each other and *do* have sex? The only thing we all have in common is that we're not straight. And am I an L or a B myself? Or maybe a Q, for the sake of convenience. That we are all promiscuous is no longer a fact, based on research among four million people showing that 98 percent of homosexuals (men and women) have had fewer than 20 different sexual partners. 99 percent of straight people score the same number. So, even that myth has been laid to rest.

To see myself as part of the LGBTQ+ community would be akin to identifying with all the redheads.

I do understand, though. The voices of minorities are louder when they unite, and people need labels to make sense of things. But, above all, this creates an 'us and them' mentality. Our preference sets itself apart from the rest of the group and that is precisely what causes all the finger-pointing and pursed lips from bystanders.

Julian and I once made a work called '562.' In the video, I read 562 questions that gays are regularly asked. From 'Would you like to come to dinner? I've always wanted a lesbian couple in our circle of friends,' and 'How do you know you don't like men/women if you've never tried it?' to 'How could your parents still be proud of you?' and 'You know you're going to hell, right?'

I understand people's curiosity. I understand that people want to know how my life changed after I met Julian, and how my mother and my friends responded. I consider that to be a healthy curiosity; one that I am also guilty of, several times a day. But, many of these questions imply disapproval, and whether the question is innocent or not, many people continue to see gays as a different species. Need proof? Imagine being asked, as a straight couple, to pretend that you're not a couple because otherwise grandma will be upset. Or someone feeling the need to tell you that it's 'completely okay' to be straight. That he has 'absolutely no problem with that, at all!' What would the world look like to you, then?

However, it would be disingenuous of me to state that I noticed no differences between being with a male or female partner. I had a lot of gay friends, among whom just a few were female couples. Still, it seemed to me that falling in love with a woman required a manual that I'd have to write myself. So, I plunged headlong into the discovery of this new world. I am someone who, after booking a beach holiday, will look up what's the best way to relax on a beach. Next, I will look up the definition of 'relax' and then, after finding out that reading on a beach is relaxing, I'll ask which are the most relaxing books of the year. Just so I'll know what to do on that beach.

Take it easy, Julian often said, briefly stroking my head. As if I were an overenthusiastic puppy. She didn't call me neurotic. She kept it amiable.

I watched all episodes of *The L Word*, an American series about the lives of a group of lesbian women in Los Angeles, many of which were written by A.M. Homes, one of my favourite writers.

I was wondering if, like in the series, we should go to the Dinah Shore Weekend. Julian rolled her eyes and said there was no way I could get her to attend a women-only festival. Twenty thousand women, to be precise. I looked at the contents of my bookcase which unintentionally, and with the exception of Paul Auster, consisted mostly of women and queer writers: Jeanette Winterson, A.M. Homes, Douglas Coupland, Patricia Highsmith, Alice Walker, Audre Lorde,

Bret Easton Ellis, Michael Cunningham, Christopher Isherwood, Allen Ginsberg.

I wondered if that had been a portent or a coincidence. The fact that I always danced to Jimmy Somerville's music and Gloria Gaynor's 'I Will Survive' didn't count, because who doesn't love those? But Julian couldn't stop laughing when I told her about my first two great loves, Boy George and the vocalist of the band Europe (Those flowing blonde locks! That pink lipstick!), and yelled, 'You're sooo gay!'

Julian, the only person allowed to give me a label, always said she saw me as a gay man in a woman's body. Which suited her, because she fell for the exuberance of most gay men, but was only attracted by a feminine package.

A few months after our first meeting and as part of my 're-search,' I booked a weekend for the two of us in Berlin, where a number of lectures and events on lesbian identity were being given. Julian thought it was all very funny and willingly let herself be taken in tow. Berlin was a sweet shop of information and the first exhibition we visited, by photographer Camilla Storgaard, featured a life-size photo of 'our' porn actress, who we had briefly heard speak in Amsterdam. The world remains well-ordered.

For the entire weekend, I dragged my love around town, taking hundreds of notes on topics I wanted to write about: women who identified as men without needing surgery, Pride advocates and opponents, poc lesbians, homosexual representation in art history. Between the talks she placidly perused a biography of Peggy Guggenheim. On the last day, and two hours before our departure back to Amsterdam, I wanted to attend another workshop.

A well-known sculptor in the lesbian community was presenting a workshop called *Pussy Stübchen*. Not hindered by any knowledge of German, I had registered, only to discover on the spot that this was a translation of 'pussy sculpting.' When, upon arrival, the artist pressed a mirror and a piece of clay into our hands and showed us to the back room to undress, I stared, wide-eyed, at my wife. 'Too much information!' I whispered.

Julian kindly returned our mirrors and clay. She usually observed my explorations with amusement, but there were limits.

=

In December 1922, the English poet, writer and designer Vita Sackville-West fell madly in love with Virginia Woolf. In her own words, she became reduced to 'a thing that wants Virginia.' She was married to a diplomat called Harold Nicholson and they had an open marriage, in which they both maintained same-sex relationships. The day she met Virginia, she wrote to her husband, 'I've rarely taken such a fancy to anyone, and I think she likes me. At least, she asked me to Richmond where she lives. Darling, I have quite lost my heart.'

Vita became Virginia's muse and inspired the ground-breaking book Orlando, a novel about a young nobleman at the court of Queen Elizabeth I, who wakes up one day and has changed gender. For the next three hundred years he inhabits a female body.

Vita's son, Nigel Nicolson, called the book 'the longest and most charming love letter in literature, in which she (Virginia

Woolf) explores Vita, weaves her in and out of the centuries, tosses her from one sex to the other, plays with her, dresses her in furs, lace and emeralds, teases her, flirts with her, drops a veil of mist around her.'

Their relationship lasted almost twenty years, until 28 March 1941, when Woolf, driven by an all-consuming depression, filled the pockets of her dress with stones and drowned herself in the River Ouse.

Nigel Nicolson published a book containing more than five hundred letters that the women wrote to each other during their lifetime. After the suicide, Vita wrote a letter to Virginia's husband Leonard: '[Virginia was] the loveliest mind and spirit I ever knew, immortal both to the world and us who loved her ... This is not a hard letter to write as you will know something of what I feel and words are unnecessary. For you I feel a really overwhelming sorrow, and for myself a loss which can never diminish.'

*I'm longing for a world where
everybody can be more relaxed into
doing what they want to do.*

In conversation with Sam Bettens
Et Alors? Magazine

WE MOVED QUICKLY THROUGH LIFE. IN ALL AREAS: THE practical, the big dreams for the future, but also the personal ones. When I met Julian, her name was Paulien. A name she hated, and found too feminine and bland to capture her personality. One night, at a dinner with Renate, she again mentioned how badly she thought the name suited her. I asked what she would like to be called.

'Julian,' she said without hesitation. 'I've always thought that to be such a beautiful name.'

I marvelled at how genuinely disappointed she sounded.

'But, why not change it, then?' I said. 'If that's what you really want, from now on your name will be Julian.'

Renate nodded in agreement.

'Yes,' said Julian, 'it can actually be that simple.'

'Anything is possible,' I said.

=

For weeks after her death, I am unable to leave my bed and only get up to use the toilet and to soak in the bathtub for hours. My muscles are rigid and only hot water brings some relief.

In the last week before her death, Julian was so far gone, so unreachable and in so much pain that I hoped she would be allowed to leave soon. I began to imagine that I would find her again after she died. At that moment, too much energy went into being sick, but all that would come back afterwards. People sometimes claim they can feel their departed loved ones around them. That expectation had settled in my head: once she was gone, I would find her again. She would assist me.

I stare at the ceiling and I don't feel or see anything. I talk to her out loud but the sound dissolves into the void. I wander from room to room and lie on the floor where her sickbed had been. I don't see anything, I don't hear anything, I don't feel anything.

Bereavement hallucinations occur in 30 to 60 percent of people who have lost their partner. Neurologist Oliver Sacks has called it a 'reassuring and positive phenomenon' that plays an important role in the grieving process. According to Freud, it's how the human brain revolts against mourning. He calls it a 'hallucinatory desire psychosis.' Because grief is so painful, denying it is easier than trying to integrate it into your life. But, I was not even allowed a hallucination. She's gone, she's never coming back, and this will never be okay.

Between 1901 and 1907, the physician Duncan MacDougall conducted a number of experiments to weigh the human soul. He argued that the soul must be present in the body as a measurable, spatial substance since it could contain a whole, individual personality. MacDougall had designed a specialised weighing scale-cum-bed upon which he would comfortably install dying people while waiting for them to expire. He noted down not only the exact time of death but also the difference in weight around that time. He accounted for the loss of fluids and oxygen in his calculations. His conclusion was that the soul weighs 21 grams.

I wander from one room to another, searching for her 21 grams.

A lot of people are still stuck on the 'why?'
Why are you a woman, why
are you a man, why are you gay?
However, there is no 'why' to begin with.
It's a reality that needs no explanation
because it's about love.

In conversation with Greg McGoon
Et Alors? Magazine

MANY VOICES IN THE GAY COMMUNITY HAVE SPOKEN OUT against marriage equality. Arguments like 'Why would you want to be like everyone else?' and 'Why would you want to conform?' have some validity, yet I disagree. For us, it was not about being able to be like everyone else, but about having the same rights. To this day, there are still eleven countries where homosexuality is punishable by death. Homosexuality is still criminalised in nearly 70 countries, with sanctions ranging from corporal punishment to life imprisonment. In 2017 a sickening YouTube clip, in which gay men were thrown off a tower, went viral.

Pretending we weren't a couple was not an option. I loved my wife and wanted to hold her hand when we walked down the street. Just like any other couple in love. We were aware that, in this way, there would inevitably be a lot of countries we'd never be able to visit.

In a world where we weren't allowed to marry in 172 countries, I believed it was very important to do it anyhow. Because it ought to be a human right.

And because it was romantic, and we were, too.

Whenever a new country allowed same-sex couples to marry, I felt the urge to uncork a bottle and do a joyful dance, unless I was called to order by a stern-looking Julian. Why cheer every time for something that ought to be the norm? Who thinks themself so terribly important that they may judge whether or not I can marry the woman of my life? She couldn't help bringing that up each time, but fortunately there'd be drinks afterwards.

One year after our first meeting, we decided to get married. It went something like this:

Her: 'I would love to marry you. I think you'll look great in a white dress. And I want to stay with you forever.'

Me: 'Yay!'

We decided to get married using a ritual that we had pieced together ourselves. That part was important: that it was by us, and for us. We rented a house with a pool in France, and our best friends flew over for sunshine, love, and languor. On the last-but-one-day of our holiday we would get married. Those were wonderful days. My mother kept the refrigerator continually stocked and it was sweltering hot, leaving us with barely enough energy for lazing by (and in) the pool, eating, and talking. It was the summer when 'Call Me Maybe' was playing constantly on the radio and there was always one of us singing the song. I thought to myself that there was quite a bit of diversity around that pool. Boys who had once been girls, non-binary people, men who liked to wear dresses. In short: friends.

On the day of the wedding I sat in a room with Renate and my mother. I had bought a white, crocheted dress. No shoes, because I always wanted to get married barefoot. Two pigeons sipping from a cocktail glass (a craft project I'd spent hours completing at home) perched on my head. Julian waited in another room with Richard and Elard. The first one morphed into Jennifer, our wedding official.

Julian said her wedding vows and wept. I cried. Everyone was shedding tears, possibly provoked by the rivers of champagne we had been testing 'for quality' in the days before the wedding.

Although we would later marry four more times as a performance, this ceremony always remained the real marriage to us. Friends, summer, and lots of love.

=

When I've spent three weeks in bed, Jeroen and his wife Nikkie come to get me in France. They're taking me to Antwerp because I have friends there, an emotional safety net. I feel guilty about returning to Antwerp and I'm having a hard time with it. It's where I was living when I met Julian. Now that she's gone, I'm going back. I feel like a traitor who has learned nothing from the past seven years. Who unthinkingly returns to the familiar. The truth is, I don't know where else to go, because wherever I go, I will have to take myself with me.

The day before my departure, I reorganise our two suitcases. All her clothes had been washed before she became ill and no longer carry her scent. Still, I can't get rid of them and plan to leave one suitcase with my mother. I sit on the floor and make piles. At intervals my body starts to protest and I lie on my back, staring at the ceiling until I can sit up straight again. I pick up one thing after another and let each object break my heart a little more. The leather wristbands she used to wear, I'll take with me. Her two wedding suits, one blue and one black, to match my outfits, are left behind. Why do I find so little of her in the objects strewn around me? Objects are said to carry meaning in troubled times, and I'm aware that I'm searching for some kind of magic. But I can't find any. Everything is cold and impersonal. I put all her clothes in her suitcase. Along with my New York wedding outfit and all the notebooks containing our future plans. When a scrap of paper falls out of one of the diaries, I am transported back to that pool, that house and our friends. It's the sheet on which she wrote her marriage vows and as I read it, I can hear her voice.

Darling, from the moment our eyes met, I knew that one day we would be facing each other like this. It's not as if we need to marry to know that we love each other, or to know that I want to spend the rest of my life with you. We are getting married today, just because we can. You are the most beautiful, sweetest, finest, and most remarkable woman there is. You give me the peace of mind to grow, and bring out the best in me. Every morning when I wake up next to you, I am the happiest person in the world and there is nothing about you that I would like to change. I love you more every second we're together. I promise I will take care of you and love you, as much as I can. And that hopefully I can make you even happier than you are now. I am so grateful to know you and that you want to be with me. I hope it is forever. As far as I'm concerned it will be.

After reading her vows, I throw up everything I had struggled to eat that morning.

Be patient and trust yourself.
Look for others who are like you and
don't get caught up so much
on those who aren't.

In conversation with Jase Peeples
Et Alors? Magazine

'I DON'T WANT TO WORK FOR A BOSS ANYMORE AND I WANT TO live by the Mediterranean,' Julian said when I asked her about her dreams. Two years after we found each other, we'd sat down to discuss them. We were on vacation at my mother's place in France. Julian had just returned from a measuring project in Ghana and was exhausted. As romantic as her job abroad sounded, in reality the team had been working seven days a week to get everything done within the expected timeframe. After twenty days in Africa, she was in dire need of a break. During the day we lounged on the beach with piles of books, living on fruit, grilled vegetables and baguettes, and in the evenings we took long walks on the beach. We slept till late in the day and put fresh, white sheets on the bed daily, because it felt so wonderful to crawl under them at night.

Julian had struggled for some time with the work she was doing. The projects usually took place in regions where there was a lot of poverty and where land expansion had an enormous ecological impact. The measuring equipment disturbed underwater life and the noise and commotion made the fish move away, leaving the local population barely able to provide for essential needs. The older she got, the more she knew she no longer wanted to be part of it.

Lying on our stomachs, in the sand, we made a list of our options. Julian sketched a map of the Mediterranean. North Africa was disqualified because we were gay. Eastern Europe was too cold. If we ended up emigrating, then it would preferably be to a warm country. Malta was too small; in Greece it would probably take us a long time to learn the language, and the South of France was too expensive. An hour later we had a plan to travel to the southern coast of Spain. If we didn't find 'it' there, then Italy was second on the list.

The financial plan would require more courage. Julian could take on calculation assignments, which she could do from home, and we would be fully committed to expanding *Et Alors?* We wanted to publish more regularly and see if we could find advertisers. We should be able to get by with very little. But, she would no longer be working for a boss, we would live in a warm country and we'd always be together. If we wanted to travel, we would list our home on Airbnb.

Two weeks later we were on a plane to Seville.

=

Renate has arranged for me to rent an apartment from an acquaintance in Antwerp for a few weeks. My mother has made arrangements for herself in the neighbourhood. She will keep me company as long as I feel it's necessary. Each day I cautiously move around my temporary home. Since she's been gone, there's something in every room. I can't hear or see it, but I know it's watching me. It watches every movement and listens to every thought. It follows me on the street, hides around corners, disguises itself as a building, a town square, or a coffee bar. I'm walking on eggshells. Because, as soon as I make a wrong move or look in a certain direction, it rushes me. It knocks the air out of my lungs, sits on my chest, and sucks all the life out of me. Tears stream down my face. I gasp and double over with pain. It hits me so suddenly that anticipating it is impossible. So, I keep as quiet as possible. I look around me as little as possible. Until I catch myself reminiscing, and it starts all over again. Every single day. From the moment I open my eyes until I reluctantly fall asleep. After a few weeks it feels like I've been beaten black and blue. With fracture lines that get deeper every time. Without any possibility of healing.

Happiness is a moment in time, finding meaning is a constant. Grief upends this structure and has only one focus: the self. It's a matter of survival. Reality is a lurking predator that, triggered by the glance of a stranger, a string of musical notes from a car, or a scent that wasn't there before, will shred the carefully-constructed screen between the self and the world to bits. Most of the time I can't even place them, these involuntary memories.

Joan Didion, who lost both her husband and her child within a year, writes about the 'vortex,' the whirlwind that catches up with her as soon as she sees something that reminds her of her loved ones, and that leaves her in tears.

Some describe grief as a tsunami which pulls you under at unexpected moments. As if you were drowning. In *A Grief Observed*, C.S. Lewis compares it to fear: the same agitation, stomach turning, and need to swallow excess saliva. I don't feel fear. I feel this invisible thing that's squeezing my throat. That leaves me bruised. Without a grip on myself, or on life.

If I have to avoid everything that reminds me of Julian, then I can never leave my bed. The world is one, huge minefield. Sometimes, I am brave and go out in pursuit of the memories, determined to exorcise a favourite restaurant, bookshop, or gallery. Like a driver who gets back behind the wheel as soon as possible after the accident. It makes no difference. Her absence is ubiquitous and I am the one who takes her everywhere. Who transforms every space into time. Places we've been bring back memories. Places we haven't been make me cry for everything she's missing out on.

*I would like to create an entire world
of fluorescent beauty. I want to remind
the world that there are no limits.*

In conversation with Anto Christ
Et Alors? Magazine

OUR PLAN WAS TO FLY TO SEVILLE, STAY THERE FOR A FEW days, then rent a car and drive down the coast. The fact that it was August, and we were in an area known as the frying pan of Andalusia,' had not been considered. From ten o'clock in the morning, one could barely move. So, we'd drag ourselves to the nearest terrace bar, from where we'd point out the city's best spots in the travel guide, unable to muster up the energy to actually visit them. The second day, the waiter no longer asked for our order but put iced tea with extra ice cubes on the table. Every few hours he brought out something to eat. Large bowls of fresh gazpacho and bread, almond cookies, olives, and some meatless paella his wife had prepared for us. We read travelogues by Paul Theroux and Edith Wharton and watched people with lolling tongues and sweat-stained clothes pass by our table. At night, wooden planks were placed on the floor of the café and the owners' youngest son danced flamenco, which involved shrieking, singing, and shouting. Later we would see a lot more flamenco, but to me it could never rival what we'd seen then.

In those early days, when we just surrendered to everything that was happening.

After four days, our bodies had more or less adjusted to the heat and we kissed the café people goodbye. Our rental car turned out to be a fiery red Fiat 500, and we drove across the Spanish mountains looking like a giant M&M.

We were on the road for ten days. From Seville to the Portuguese border, and then up the entire Spanish coast. Singing, because 'Get Lucky' by Daft Punk and Pharrell Williams was a big hit at the time and played on the radio every half hour.

We've come too far to give up who we are
So let's raise the bar and our cups to the stars

On the seventh day we drove up the mountain from the seaboard to Frigiliana. Julian had the giggles because I felt the car was moving vertically and kept both feet on the accelerator. Reaching the top, we looked at each other and knew we had found it. The heavy scent of jasmine blossom, the white houses with the sea in the distance. We parked the car and entered the first of two hotels in the village. We were lucky, said the lady behind the desk, someone has just cancelled. We lay down on the bed and looked at the sea. 'Here we are,' she said.

=

Looking out the window, I see a nursery school. I know when to avoid the mothers collecting their offspring. I have a hard time with people who have children. With couples. With people who have homes. With people who have pets. And with those mothers, looking silently happy on the other side of my window. A woman I've never met writes to me that she lost her husband three years earlier, and that she's been walking around in a haze, ever since. 'Fortunately, I have my children,' she says. 'Without them, there would be nothing left to live for, I would no longer be here.' After that letter, I'm staring in front of me for hours. I wonder if people realise what they are saying. I wish I had a child. Then, I could still nurture something. Then, there would still be a future.

When I'm not reading, I try to answer as many emails and letters as possible. There are hundreds of them pouring into my inbox every day. Contact with the world outside my cocoon is of the essence, but how do you explain something like this? It soon becomes clear that few people know what this feels like, so lazily reach for clichés.

'She's still with you.'

'Your love will endure forever.'

'You two did have some great experiences together, didn't you?'

For the first time in my life, I resent not being understood. How do I explain that I'm sitting behind my laptop shivering, with chattering teeth? Chilled to the bone despite my four sweaters. At times I'm shaking so hard that my fingers slide off the keys, and I keep having to swallow down bile all the time. My head has turned into my body's enemy, and it feels like I'm about to break. At night I go looking for her against my better judgement. Feeling my way in the dark, I walk from room to room with the walls for support. I ask her to give me a sign that she is alright. So that at least one of us is okay. I don't hear anything, I don't feel anything, and I crawl back into bed, numb with cold.

=

In 1948, the American playwright Tennessee Williams had a one-night stand with truck driver Frank Merlo. Frank became the love of his life. A few weeks after meeting, the couple moved in together. Merlo quit his job to devote himself to his partner's career. Williams, dependent on drugs and alcohol in the past, was finally able to focus on writing. Merlo cooked, cleaned, acted as a chauffeur, and mentored him through his play, *The Rose Tattoo*. He encouraged him during the difficult writing process of *Cat on a Hot Tin Roof*, which Williams feared would never surpass the success of *A Streetcar Named Desire*. The play earned him his second Pulitzer.

In 1962 Merlo was diagnosed with lung cancer. He died a year later. 'He had a gift for creating a life and, when he ceased to be alive, I couldn't create a life for myself,' Williams wrote in *Memoirs*, and he was pulled into a maelstrom of alcohol and drugs. None of his subsequent plays had the quality of his earlier work. He died alone at Hotel Elysée in New York on February 25, 1983.

=

I put my emotions under a magnifying glass and discover different ways of crying. Different kinds of tears. There is the crying of loss and emptiness. Of finality and of 'never again.' It rises up from the depths of my belly and sounds like a beast in agony. I can't help but surrender and gasp for air until it subsides. Those tears are the worst.

There is the crying of self-pity. Long sobs. Because I no longer have a home, because all those beautiful plans have been cancelled. Because I'll be alone for the rest of my life. Self-pity remains a difficult concept. I grew up with a mother who, every time I cried, asked me if I had a good reason for it. If you cried for no good reason, it was called whining.

There is the crying brought on by the reality check, when I recognise myself in what Roland Barthes in his *Mourning Diary* calls: 'A devastated person prey to presence of mind.' Expecting her to be there when I wake up, knowing she's not, but still looking for her anyway. Thinking for a split second that she has just stepped out of the room and will return later. The moment I open my mouth to say something only to realise she's not there. Those are the tears that run down my cheeks without warning. From shock.

'There's no limit to one's stupidity,' wrote Leonard Woolf, finding himself still looking out the window, expecting to see his wife walk across the garden, after Virginia's suicide.

On my way to get groceries, I always try to walk through the shopping centre. When I feel a crying fit coming on, I run into a shop, grab something off the racks and lock myself, sobbing, into a fitting room. The mirrors come in handy, to make me more or less presentable afterwards. It's an illusion, because I'm not one of those people whose tears roll down a beautiful, impassive face. When I cry, my forehead wrinkles, my nose turns red, and my eyes shrink. My upper lip swells to the point where I resemble a rubber duck. I'm an ugly crier and I keep hoping that, at some point, I'll be done crying. That there'll be no tears left.

How many tears does one have, I wonder? Every day, litres of water. Where does that keep coming from, and do I have to drink to make up for it? I've rarely cried in the past seven years. Except, a few times, tears of happiness. Tears inadvertently welling up when I looked at her. Like that time at the beach, when I lay drowsily reading on a towel. I watched her swim further away from me. Just before I thought she might be going too far out, she turned around. A big smile on her face. Her arm shot up in the air, and she waved before swimming back to me. Tears came to my eyes. It was full-on happiness. Or, was it fear? Not a single memory of her has remained untainted. Every event is shrouded in a mist of knowledge, takes on a different colour, once you know how the story ends. And, my memory is playing tricks on me.

I read somewhere that babies only cry real tears after two or three months. That women cry more than men (5.3 times versus 1.4 times a month) and that their crying spells last four times longer, on average. Especially between seven and ten in the evening. Tears can be a release-valve for the mind, or a cry for help. They produce endorphins; a pain-relieving hormone that can be compared to a gentle massage or shower. Crying in response to emotions only occurs in humans. In 2011, an Indian girl was reported to be weeping stones. Every day she cried twelve to twenty-five mini-rocks. It didn't hurt. Kura Nitya puzzled scientists.

Mathieu Trudel, partner of the international DJ Takami Nakamoto, disappeared in early 2016. After a few days, his dead body was found in Canada.

Nakamoto contacted photographer Maurice Mikkers and the two started a project about the fear of disappearance, and the grief of mourning. It resulted in the music video *Where Is Mawt*.

Nakamoto kept his tears in test tubes and put them under the microscope. Mikkers filmed the crystallisation process. Together they edited the recording so that it synced with music composed especially for the project. 'The feelings that this tragedy aroused in us should not be lost. By making a music video together, we turned Takami's tears and memories into something that immortalises Mathieu,' Mikkers told *Vice*.

Nowhere do I read whether or not you can cry too much, causing you to dry up like a shrivelled old potato.

I guess technology isn't ready for pancake teleportation.

In conversation with Niels Peeraer
Et Alors? Magazine

ME: DO YOU THINK THERE ARE CRICKETS IN SOUTHERN SPAIN?

Her: I don't know. But if you want, I can buy one of those little noise boxes. And, when I say 'shh …' while closing the lid, it will look like I've tamed them.

Me: A Spanish cricket whisperer.

=

I find myself revisiting music from when I was twenty. I lie on the bed, and turn up Faith No More and the Red Hot Chili Peppers so loud it makes my ears ring. I bounce across the living room to the sound of Rage Against The Machine. 'Killing in the name of!!!'

Am I searching for that time when my life still lay ahead of me, when everything seemed to be extremely complicated but actually wasn't at all? I remember long-forgotten events I haven't told anyone about in years. Like the time Herman Brood invited me to his birthday party and I brought a friend because I was too shy to go alone. When he asked me up to his room, I said she could go in my place. After all, she had a crush on him. Later that evening she came to tell me, with a deep wrinkle in her forehead, that he had taken his dentures out. I couldn't stop laughing and I was so glad that it hadn't been me in that room. Later on he gave me his jacket, which I in turn passed on to a writer friend who was a big fan of Brood's.

Or, like the time I decided to drop out of school because I thought everyone was boring and stupid, and I got on a bus to Alsace to help with the grape harvest. For two weeks I drank litres of wine and danced to French chansons. My mother let me get it out of my system and then took me back to school.

Or the time I was the only girl to drive to Paris with a group of friends for a gay party at the Bataclan. Since women weren't allowed, they'd dressed me up as a drag queen. In high heels, and with a gigantic wig and exuberant eyebrows, I towered above the scantily-clad crowd in leather trousers and speedos. I don't believe no one noticed, but I think they just found it amusing.

Julian recognised herself in the story of how, when I was little, I wanted to be on every plane I saw flying overhead. That I wanted to walk through every intriguing door to see what lay beyond it. That I drank every potion that said 'Drink me!' And she followed.

Curiosity is the most beautiful thing you can cultivate. Always be curious, never be afraid to ask questions and try to follow your heart.

In conversation with David Weissman
Et Alors? Magazine

IT WAS THE END OF AUGUST WHEN WE FLEW BACK HOME. WE decided to return to Frigiliana a few months later, to check if the weather would still be nice, and because we hoped to find a home.

In southern Spain, winter had not yet started in November, and the village was even more beautiful than we remembered. This time my mother came and joined us from France. With her sixth sense for good and bad vibes, she had once strongly advised me against moving into a certain apartment. Later, it turned out that a man had murdered his family there, with an axe. We didn't expect to encounter this kind of extreme story, but if we decided to settle down, her opinion was important anyway.

My mother, too, lost her heart as soon as she drove her car up the mountain, and from day one we were lucky enough to meet Scott, a wonderful estate agent who would later become a friend as well. He showed us three houses: the first one had no view, the second was too creepy (not an axe murderer, but probably something similar), the third house clicked as soon as we crossed the threshold. It was built in a spiral shape. A small cellar all the way at the bottom, stairs to the kitchen, stairs to the bathroom, stairs to the living room, stairs to the most fantastic terrace we'd ever seen . Sea view included. A snail shell. That the house was in terrible condition was something we had overlooked. The ocean view and the scent of oranges had blinded us, and a few hours after the viewing, Scott opened a bottle of champagne to celebrate us moving into his village.

Moving to Spain made for an exciting but stressful time. Fortunately, our yen for adventure overcame most of the negative aspects. Nevertheless, it remained challenging. We would, for instance, be completely dependent on each other. No job outside the home, no friends. Just each other. Julian fantasised about all the things she would do when she had the time. She would make a better website for *Et Alors?* We would scrutinise and implement all our ideas. She would learn to film so that I could make all the shorts I had in my head. We would become a production company. It would be called Eat The Carrot Productions, she said enthusiastically. After the donkey that chases the carrot dangling in front of it. She wouldn't chase the carrot; she would eat it. This instant. With ravenous appetite. We had a lot of imagination, but we also knew that it was solely up to us whether everything would work out.

=

Since the day she died, a month ago, I've been writing her letters. Somehow, it makes a lot of sense. I have a notebook with a picture of *Les Mariés* de la Tour Eiffel. Bought at the Centre Pompidou, at the time of our Paris wedding. Julian loved the goat with the violin. Letters, every day, constantly.

Love, today I washed my hair. I didn't cry between 8:00 a.m. and 9:34 a.m. I ate an orange.

I notice how small my life is. How I have to learn to walk again, and how every day, sometimes every hour even, is a victory. It's wearing me out. How much time do I need to get used to this second-class life? This is not what I chose. This isn't even Plan B. This is a plan with a letter that hasn't even been invented yet. Probably never will be invented.

I try to organise my days, to find a rhythm that is predictable, because the slightest change throws me off balance. Me, the one who literally lived for change. If, in the past we didn't have enough time, I now have way too much of it. Long days in which I sometimes notice, with a start, that I've been staring at my hands for hours. Or, that the tea I thought I'd just brewed has gone cold. I'm getting so tired of the sadness, of that raw aloneness. 'Try to live life well,' said Aristotle. But, how?

I get up at six because I want to be as tired as possible at night. The first thing I do is meditate. Or attempt to meditate. Sometimes I succeed, and then it envelops my days in a light, protective layer. Easy to puncture, but a soothing cover nonetheless. If I don't succeed, I step into the day as an open wound. I paint the nails of one hand and have no patience left to do the other.

I make tea and slice fruit for breakfast. Sometimes my mind wanders to other things, like the hysterical dreams I'm having about elephants on a Ferris wheel, and about drowning in a bathtub full of apples, but there always comes a moment when I suddenly freeze. My knife in midair, my legs limp. The moment it sinks in once more: I'm never going to do this for her again. I lean my forehead against the cabinet and try to relax. Sometimes it works, and when it doesn't, I get up from the kitchen floor an hour later.

I remember one of the most moving paragraphs from Isherwood's *A Single Man*, where he describes how his main character George feels an abrupt and brutal landslide every morning at the bottom of the stairs: 'It is here that he stops and knows, with a sick newness, almost like the first time: Jim is dead. Is dead.'

I read this sentence to her once because it shook me to the core 'Never die, will you?' I asked her then.

'I will never die,' she replied, laughing.

If you can go to a place where it's encouraged to be loving and to be positive, then that's the place you have to go to, to be yourself and to be free.

In conversation with Ted Rogers
and Ki Price
Et Alors? Magazine

THE MOVE TO SPAIN WAS, OF COURSE, LESS IDYLLIC THAN WE'D expected. We hadn't yet mastered the language. Frigiliana was scorching hot. The steps in the village, where there's no driving, were higher and steeper than before. Our house was less than half the size we remembered. Everything was covered in dust, as the roof terrace had collapsed since the last time we were there, and all the debris lay in the bathroom, which now had no roof. Julian got an electric shock when she switched the light on.

This was not how we wanted it. Should we go back? Ten minutes and hundreds of questions later, we had changed clothes, washed our faces, and were on our way to the restaurant we had seen at a beach on the way over. Everything would turn out fine, we said. Didn't it always?

Our house became even more of a ruin as soon as the renovation work started. All the walls were opened up, to install new water and electricity wiring, partitions had been torn down, the kitchen was ripped out and moved upstairs next to the terrace. Scott, our estate agent, had introduced us to Martin, whose grandfather had done the first renovation of our house, half a century ago. Give me three weeks, he had said with great certainty. I didn't believe a word of it, as we had been endlessly warned about the Spaniards' *mañana* mentality.

Exactly three weeks later, we were sweeping up the dust, leaving our rental apartment and moving into our house.

Given all the steps in the village, our move was done by Paco and his donkey. The first night we spent there, we were jolted awake by a deafening clatter. It turned out to be the bin man, pulling a gigantic bin on a pallet through the streets by a rope, and throwing the rubbish bags into it.

The houses in Frigiliana are built like jigsaw puzzles. Next door to us lived Antonio (most of the men in the village were called either Antonio or Paco, so you had about a 50 percent chance of addressing someone by the right name), who had part of his bathroom underneath our patio. Half of our living room was above his kitchen. The other half was taken up by the other neighbours. A messy Escher, Julian called the architectural style, suppressing her preference for order and symmetry. Once a day, at exactly ten a.m., we were overwhelmed by the smell of washing powder. Half an hour later, one pair of underpants, one vest and two socks were hanging from the clothesline on Antonio's terrace. Every single day. We wondered about how many sets he owned.

Like our neighbour, all the older men in the village were incredibly neat. The creases in their trousers and the short sleeves of their shirts were pressed into place with military precision. Most of them walked either ramrod straight, or with a stick. They all wore hats. They dressed in shades ranging from beige to tan. Every morning at eight they took a cognac at the Virtudes bar. To take the edge off the day, I imagined. Then, they took a walk around the village before alighting on the benches in front of the pharmacy. Tourists were shooed away. It was their bench. They talked incessantly, their chatter recalling a flock of birds. What they said was unintelligible because of the broad accent. Every day, from morning to night. What do they still have to tell each other? I wondered. 'They remind me of us,' Julian said, dubbing them mature loiterers.

The younger generation of men was possibly even better groomed than the old guard. A mania for shaving raged, and all boys between the ages of seventeen and twenty-five only had hair on their heads. Their faces, legs, arms, chest: everything was mirror-smooth. Some also shaved off their eyebrows. They were short in stature (genetic), broad-shouldered (daily workout) and had glowing skin (body lotion). Many worked either in construction or agriculture. The contrast with Julian was hilarious. Before we'd migrated she had asked me if I would mind terribly if she stopped shaving her legs? She absolutely loathed doing it and the hairs often grew in, leading to itchy bumps. It was completely fine with me. She was beautiful as she was. With or without hairy legs. In Frigiliana, the men looked from her legs to her breasts and back. Confusion reigned.

During the annual Mardi Gras, no one was bothered by any gender restrictions. The waiters at Virtudes, dressed up as Native American squaws, poured San Miguel beer without batting an eye, unhampered by their gigantic fake breasts and flesh-coloured tights, despite the temperature reaching 35°C outside. Half of the men in the pageant wore dresses. Some had moustaches. The parade's most enchanting attraction was Paco from the flower shop. He provided wreaths for funerals and floral décor for weddings and wore an apron for work, even though he only sold flowers and plants made from plastic. Paco was gay and in full drag during Carnival. In platform-soled shoes, he towered over the villagers and, wearing a regal expression, showered his subjects with glitter.

We watched the world from our roof terrace.

'Look,' said Julian, with a gesture that encompassed the sea, our house, myself, and Antonio's underpants, 'Everything I ever wanted. I am the happiest person in the world.'

=

I got a tattoo. The number 9122010, the date we met, above a black inverted triangle, originally one of the badges of homosexuality during the Second World War. Between 1933 and 1945, an estimated 100,000 homosexuals were arrested under Section 175 of the German Code, prohibiting homosexuality. More than 50,000 people were imprisoned, and hundreds were sentenced to castration. It is estimated that 15,000 gays were sent to the concentration camps where an inverted triangle was attached their clothing. A pink triangle for male homosexuals, but also for perpetrators of sex crimes like rape, pedophilia, and bestiality. The black triangle was used for sexworkers, alcoholics, conscientious objectors and

– although there was no structured prosecution policy in existence – lesbians, who were locked up in concentration camps under the category of 'anti-social element.'

In the 1970s, the triangle was reclaimed by the gay movement in the fight for equal rights.

Above the tattooed number on my arm: JULIAN. Egyptians repeated the names of the dead in writing because they believed that, every time you read, write, or heard their names, their soul would light up. I grasped at every bit of hope, no matter how far-fetched, as if it were a lifeline.

I know I can only affect my little corner of things, and part of that is fighting for my own human right to just be, and to go through the world. Step by step.

In conversation with Ivan Coyote
Et Alors? Magazine

I HAVE A TODDLER'S TASTE. IN A STORE I'M MAGNETICALLY drawn to the rack with the sequins, glitter, and stars, and I love everything that's pink and has palm trees, flamingos, and hearts on it. My wife would roll her eyes in jest whenever I held up a dress printed with bananas. Don't let me stop you, she'd say. But in the end, I usually opted for black. In Andalusia my love for colour resurfaced. The more clashing, the better, and my floral dresses and profusion of beads and bracelets stood out strikingly against the village women's sombre garb. Ancient, bent, and timeless ladies who told us stories about the horrors that Frigiliana had to endure over the years.

Our favourite local was María. She lived on our street and no one could tell us her age. It didn't really matter. We met her on a morning walk through the village. As we were passing the church, a very old woman came running out of the building at full speed. In rapid Spanish, tinged with the broad dialect of the region, she tried to explain something to us we didn't understand. I eyed the church in a panic, because so much drama could only be the result of a major fire. Or, maybe someone had been murdered? In the church! Disheartened, but no less loud, she finally grabbed Julian's hand and pulled her into the church. With hand gestures she made it clear that the window needed to be opened. She herself was too stooped to reach that high. Julian opened the window and María gave us a little shove: We were free to leave. Back in the square we looked at each other in bewilderment, still feeling the adrenaline rush from an expected disaster that never materialised. It was the beginning of our friendship with María. We shared our initial misgivings with her, about moving to a small, and extremely Catholic, Spanish village. As two women. As a couple. María looked at us and nodded understandingly. Then she dismissed the whole issue with a 'God makes no mistakes.' I pondered how this perspective could resolve wars.

María made an effort to talk more slowly, for our benefit. Quite an honour, apparently, were it not for the fact that she treated us as if we were retarded. The more our Spanish improved, the more delight María displayed. And, the more kisses we received as we passed by her house. A ritual that we underwent on a daily basis, as she was invariably sat on a chair in her doorway, whether we went out early in the morning or late at night. One time, Julian got up out of bed to check if she was still there at three in the morning. 'The door is closed,' she said upon returning, 'She's asleep.'

One day, as we were on our way to the beach, laden with books and towels, she jumped up towards Julian and pulled at her elbow, which was at eye level for her. She put two weathered hands on my wife's face and said, 'You are so very pretty. I could eat you.' She then let go of Julian and looked at me. 'And you're not bad either,' she said with significantly less enthusiasm.

Julian couldn't stop laughing. 'You should have seen your face!'

=

The press requests keep coming in. Because of the visibility prompted by our 22 project, her passing was big news. I thank everyone for their interest, but say that I'm unable to think coherently. Jeroen, however, convinces me otherwise. 'You've lost everything,' he says. 'Your wife, your future, your home, and your work. You need some help.' He suggests I should talk to someone I trust, someone capable of shaping my confused utterances into readable sentences. I decide to talk to two journalists from the largest Belgian newspaper. I tell them how disenchanted I am with life; I wonder why I met the love of my life, and why she is no longer here. Is it a test of character or did I do something terrible to deserve this? I can only conclude that life is neither given to one, nor taken away. It just is. And that's very sobering. I also tell them that I promised her I would write a book and that I have already started fulfilling that promise.

The day of the diagnosis was when I started writing. Firstly lists. The pills she had to take. The little things she said. The doctor's words. I did it to try and comprehend what was being said, what was happening. After her death, the lists became memories. Descriptions of our life together. It was my way of getting to grips with the situation. For me, writing is a combination of remembering and of trying to let reality sink in. In the past I would have added: and of leaving something behind. By now, I have lost that illusion, as well. 'Man reckons with immortality and forgets to reckon with death,' wrote Milan Kundera. Once upon a time I considered immortality important. The idea that one can leave something behind always appealed to me. A year ago, however, Julian and I had been sitting on a bench in Central Park, next to two teenage girls. 'Who is Michael Jackson?' one of them asked the other. 'That puts everything in perspective,' said Julian.

The day the article appears, I am shocked to see myself on the front page of the newspaper. So pale, and unlike myself. Without a smile, without any sparkle in my eyes. Two days later, I have already received calls from six publishers who want to publish my book, and I note that this is the first positive future outlook since Julian's diagnosis. Saskia De Coster, one of my favourite writers, recommends her publisher. Twenty-four hours later, Marscha and Daniël from Das Mag are on my doorstep in Antwerp. An hour later, I have decided that they are the people I want to work with.

That night, unable to sleep, I create a structural representation of our life on the wall. From our meeting in 2010 to her death in 2018, every memory represented by a Post-it note. When I'm done, I sit on the floor and gaze at the most important period of my life. Then, the sun rises, comes in through the window, bounces off the lamp and projects a rainbow above the hundred bits of paper.

Since her death, I no longer believe in magic. But, sometimes it's hard not to.

=

Gloria Joseph is an activist, writer and professor who has been committed to the fight against racism, sexism, and homophobia for more than 60 years. In 2016 she wrote *The Wind Is Spirit: The Life, Love and Legacy of Audre Lorde*. The biography is composed of witty reminiscences and stories from the family and friends of her partner Audre Lorde, a renowned poet, feminist and activist. Her poems speak about her anger and rage at the civil and social inequalities she witnessed throughout her life. Her work is about both feminism and the exploitation of black female identity. Lorde emphasised the importance of intersectionality: the recognition that various, oppressive factors can be at work simultaneously, and in different ways. She explained how she had been oppressed as a woman, doubly oppressed as a black woman, and triply-oppressed as a lesbian black woman.

Before her death in 1992, Lorde had discussed the possibility of writing a biography with Joseph. In the turbulent two years before she died of breast cancer, she asked her partner to leave behind a story about what she was really like. In all her complexity. She also asked her to narrate her life so compellingly that people would be inspired to adopt her views. 'But don't make me into a myth,' she added.

Joseph wrote a biography in which more than 50 prominent writers and activists contributed their thoughts and feelings.

*I feel very blessed and grateful for the
happy life I have now, and I hope that I
have the ability to inspire others to
overcome the pain.*

In conversation with Buck Angel
Et Alors? Magazine

IN SPAIN, JULIAN WORKED AT BUILDING AN EXTREMELY ambitious website for *Et Alors?*. I was working on a hundred projects at once. I did interviews, wrote them up, and worked on new collages in the hope of creating more clarity in the world around us. We worked under the name JF. Pierets.

Works such as *The Royal Anthem*, a six-part series in which we photographed ourselves as a royal couple with sash, medals, tiara and all. We hung the portraits in haphazardly-chosen interiors, wondering whether the European custom of hanging a picture of the royal couple would still persist if the couple where straight. We eagerly awaited the first openly gay king, or queen.

According to studies, people are able to exhibit greater acceptance if they have come into contact with something. The proverbial 'only gay in the village' is accepted, because everyone knows him. Because everyone's standing in line at the bakery with him, her or them. If people have even one homosexual acquaintance, they are more likely to support equal rights. The phenomenon is known as 'contact theory' and was researched by Daniel DellaPosta, a professor at Pennsylvania State University. Being gay himself, he wanted to find out why acceptance of homosexuality had increased fivefold between 1973 and 2016. In his study *Gay Acquisitions and Attitudes Toward Homosexuality: A Conservative Test*, he states that his data analysis shows that straight people who don't have any gay friends have an increased number of prejudices. But, if you take one step up, to the level of acquaintance – knowing someone's name, having a chat with them in the street – the 'contact effect' is triggered. And, between 1973 and 2016, gradually more people had come out as gay.

DellaPosta was inspired to conduct this research by a letter from Harvey Milk. A letter that was only made public after Milk, himself a pioneer of the gay rights movement in the 1960s and 1970s, had been shot. In the letter, he encouraged people to be open about their sexuality: 'I would like to see every gay doctor come out, every gay lawyer, every gay architect come out, stand up and let the world know,' Milk said. 'That would do more to end prejudice overnight than anybody would imagine. I urge them to do that, urge them to come out. Only that way will we start to achieve our rights.'

Most of the time Julian and I would use ourselves as subjects in work that was poised somewhere between photography and theory, performance, and collage. A research-based exercise where we wanted to act as a mirror in which the viewer is confronted with his or her ideologies and assumptions, rigid or not. Fascinated by gender, identity and community, we questioned how much of one's identity is fixed, and how much of it is shaped by one's environment. And, how that affects someone's perspective on the world. In our work we tried to capture the current era, and see how it functions at the level of equal rights. We conveyed how the world is changing, evolving, and sometimes regressing. We observed and documented what was happening around us. Discovering patterns and taking responsibility, informing people about them. We were convinced that limitations are nothing but constructs and that, with enough imagination, one can transform any limiting belief from the outside.

=

'What do you want to be when you grow up?' I once asked her. It was evening, and we were lounging side by side on a blanket. It seemed like a film. Our white, Spanish house with the blue shutters and sea views. My jaw fitting perfectly into the hollow beneath her shoulder. She smelled of caramel and warm bread.

'A drummer,' she said. The day before she had watched a documentary about the Foo Fighters. My wife was very empathetic.

'What do you want to be?'

As a child I knew early on what I wanted out of life. An artist and writer, I'd said when people asked me that question. A female writer, they corrected me. No, a writer, I retorted. One word. Genderless. An activist from nursery school on. Wouldn't I rather become a nurse or a teacher? was the next question. Earnestly, I shook my head. I had, after all, won a story contest, so my calling had already been confirmed.

How sad it is that I am now writing a book that I would never have wanted to write.

By making things very fabulous and gay, I try to make eye candy to get people's attention at first. Yet, in the end my work is very dark and contains a spiky message.

In conversation with Ayakamay
Et Alors? Magazine

'DO YOU KNOW TOM AND HARRY?'

'No.'

'That's odd, since they're also gay.'

Our Danish neighbours in Frigiliana were throwing a dinner party. We had met them when we first moved into the village and by now, two years later, we had become good friends.

Someone at the table had asked us if people still reacted weirdly to two women. As a couple. We had some stories that made everyone laugh.

'But, overall, it's okay, isn't it? When it comes to human rights?'

We explained that, out of 194 countries, we were allowed to marry in only twenty-two of them. Jaws dropped. It was the umpteenth time we'd got that response.

The next morning, I woke up at five and gently woke Julian up by placing my finger on her nose.

'What if we got married everywhere we're allowed? That way we would celebrate the twenty-two countries, but we would have also pointed out that it's not allowed in the other 172.'

'Great idea, honey,' she said. And then she fell back to sleep.

The idea of 22, as we had now named the project, was set aside. That's how we did things. Julian always wanted to shelve an idea, in order to see if it would stand the test of time.

22 still remained a good idea, even after a few weeks, but Julian felt tired and had to lie down more and more often in the afternoons. I was worried. I grilled her about exactly how she was feeling. She didn't know.

One day she walked into our office crying. She had felt something in her breast. She cried with long gasps and I held her close.

'I don't wanna die.'

=

Today we would have arrived in Montevideo. For marriage number seven. After Paris, we had planned a month of pre-production for the next part of our journey. Madrid in January, after which Argentina was next on the list. Then Uruguay. Five countries in South America. Then, a stop over in California to prepare for a new batch. Travelling with the sun, so that we would get married in Iceland and Scandinavia during the summer. We had the luxury of visiting the (by now twenty-eight) most progressive countries in the world. After our last marriage, in New Zealand, we would return to the country we had chosen as our home base along the way.

What a wonderful life that was, I reflected, staring out the window at the falling snow.

In Antwerp I roam from one place to another. A week here, then two weeks on the other side of town. Sometimes a guest room, sometimes a whole apartment. My suitcase and me. I don't know where I want to live, I don't know where I want to be. I can't get warm anywhere and I spend many of my days under the covers, somewhat sheltered and detached from the world. With my iPod and Nick Cave on repeat. 'With my voice, I am calling you.' Cave's voice has this compelling tone that I can easily tolerate. The Skeleton Tree is my music to mourn to and Renate comes to pick me up to go to the cinema: the concert film Distant Sky is playing at the theatre.

I have always hated pathos and sentimentality. It makes my hair stand on end. With films or books, Julian often teased,'my sentimentality meter goes into the red.'

What strikes me about grief is that any form of sentimentality is forgiven. By me, as much as by others. People tell me that the unthinkable has happened, and my heart must be broken into a thousand pieces. I nod and the monitor doesn't budge. When someone asks me how I'm doing, I say without blinking that I'm falling apart. That I'm dying of misery. I talk about suffocating pain. About a grief that sits on my chest, oppressive and unwieldy and unrelenting. In mourning, everything is allowed and even the most pathetic imagery cannot match reality. New words must be found. Until then, I'll cry to Barry Manilow's 'Could It Be Magic' and sentimental YouTube videos of babies and puppies.

What scares me most is the finality of it all. The despair of knowing that I can never change anything about her death. She will always remain dead. She will never come back. It's the finality that makes it harrowing. No matter how much headway I make, my hope of ever getting her back is something I need to surrender to. Despair overshadows every thought and blocks all progress. Former pastor and writer Rob Bell described despair as a spiritual condition: 'It tells you that tomorrow will be just like today.'

There are, of course, other things that shape a future. I hope, for instance, to make a documentary one day. To write books. To create new visual work. But, at the root of all this lies the hope of something which I can never achieve: that I will wake up to a life that has once more assumed its proper structure. Despair and hope become one and the same emotion. A Janus head whose two faces howl with open mouths.

I'm trying to tell universal stories
because the one thing that every single
person on the planet struggles with and
what every single person wants, is the
ever-elusive true love.

In conversation with Marina Rice Bader
Et Alors? Magazine

I FOUND OUT THAT I'M GOOD AT DEALING WITH PANIC situations. After she discovered the lump in her breast, I cried with her, but quickly felt my shoulders straighten and my jaw clench. I drove down from our mountain to the nearest hospital, where I demanded they examine her on the spot.

The three days we had to wait for the results felt endless. This can't be happening to her, can it? We still have so many plans. We are so happy.

The last sip from a bottle, a dropped eyelash, seeing a rainbow, everything had always been a pretext for making a wish.

'I don't know what to wish for,' she often said. 'I already have you.'

'Wish for a hedgehog,' I would say. 'For the patio.'

We should have asked for health. In the midst of our happiness, it was the one thing we had overlooked.

It turned out that my wife had advanced breast cancer and urgently needed surgery. Additional tests were done at another clinic. The hospital looked dingy. The doctors' white shoes were stained. A cleaning lady was mopping the hallways with a bucket full of dirty water. While Julian was under the scanner, I called my mother, crying.

'She's going to get even sicker here. I can feel it.'

'Drive straight on to Antwerp,' she said.

As soon as Julian emerged from the scanner, I told her we were leaving.

'How?' she wondered.

'I'll figure something out,' I said, 'on the way.'

While she was packing our bags, I called a doctor friend in Antwerp, who in turn called a surgeon at the hospital to have her put on the emergency list. Our friends Peter and Luc said their guest room was ready for us. Those were the longest 2304 kilometres I ever drove, but I remember being especially happy that we were on the road. I was getting her to safety, I was going to make her better.

=

Today I started wearing a small spherical urn on a silver chain. Jewellery designer and friend Nico Taeymans and his wife Nadia had asked me if I'd let them design something in which I could carry Julian's ashes around with me. One afternoon of tea and tears, we had discussed the design, which I now wear on my right wrist. I feel it's exquisite, and it suits me perfectly. And her, as well.

Although I'm not convinced that these remains represent Julian's actual presence, I do treat he ashes with respect.

They are what's left of the beautiful shell that used to contain my wife. I am not grateful to that body, because it destroyed her from within. But, it was what carried her and moved her around. I now notice how, every once in a while, I gently put my hand on it. To check, against my better judgement, if I can feel her. Because the desire is so strong and so convincing that I can feel the hollow on her neck, below her hairline, under my fingertips. That I can smell the skin in the crook of her elbow. That I feel the waves of happiness washing over me as she takes my face in both hands, looks me in the eye and says, 'I love you so much. Do you know that?' That I hear her yell, 'Come play?' when she felt I was working too long.

More than five million sensory cells respond to touch and initiate the production of endorphins, a hormone that stimulates the immune system, metabolism, and aids digestion. The happiness hormone. The lack of it is sometimes referred to as 'skin hunger.' A poetic term for something that can lead to depression. For something that causes extreme stress and chronic abnormalities.

I've always loved eccentrics – because they dare to be different, because they reinvent themselves every day.

In conversation with Tim Lienhard
Et Alors? Magazine

IT WAS A RELIEF TO ARRIVE IN ANTWERP, BUT THAT RELIEF was soon quashed by the series of tests she had to undergo. For two weeks she was wheeled from one scanner to another, and each time the wait for the results was unnerving. Waiting to find out where she was on the scale of direness. She endured it all stoically, but I could see the panic in her eyes. She only cried once. It was when she'd been called away from my side in the waiting room and was subsequently made to wait for a long time in a little anteroom. Her imagination had been given so much time that, once under the scanner, she'd turned into a nervous wreck, as the doctors were able to see what was wrong, while she herself remained in the dark. It took me a long time to steady her, and I realised how hard we were both trying to put up a brave front. We talked a lot, but I didn't allow myself to panic. This resulted in a stiff neck, tight shoulders, and a state of restlessness that sometimes, when I was alone in the shower, caused me to tremble and my teeth to start chattering.

Our days fell into the same routine, and Julian used the two weeks between diagnosis and surgery to read one book after another. What is cancer? What does it do? What can you do about it yourself? As Siri Hustvedt wrote in *The Shaking Woman*, 'If I couldn't cure myself, perhaps I could at least begin to understand myself.'

I cooked healthily and we went to the gym every day, because she wanted to go into surgery as strong as possible. I followed, listened, performed, and participated. Mainly because I didn't want to be away from her for a second. We were in a state of panic, but we decided not to see it as the enemy. It took a lot of willpower. But, what was the alternative?

One breast needed to be removed. And a number of lymph nodes.

'Take them both away,' she said. 'Otherwise, I'll worry about the other one for the rest of my life.' And she didn't want a reconstruction, either; she refused to have something in her body that wasn't hers. The doctor looked surprised, but Julian remained convinced. The surgery took a long time, and the nurses patiently put up with me turning up every fifteen minutes to ask if she was okay. Meanwhile, my mother had arrived from France and was trying to calm me down. I saw my own panic reflected in her eyes.

An amputation involves drainage bottles, to drain off fluids and blood. Fragile and pale, Julian lay in the hospital bed with two bottles, one on either side, where her breasts had once been. In the recovery room she smiled at me.

'I've missed you.'

I tried not to look at the blood flowing out of her body and through the tubes. When there were visitors, I'd sit between them and the bottles, for fear that someone would bump into them and hurt her. She seemed to take it all in her stride herself, and I wished that I could have some of her sedatives.

=

Ever since the plan to write a book took shape, I live even more of my days in the past. I try to write down as much as possible, so as not to forget. I remember a childhood photo of hers. A beautiful child, in little blue dungarees and yellow rubber boots. A dark, full head of hair. It must have been taken on her grandmother's farm. In her right hand she has a plush rabbit that she took everywhere with her. She looks shyly into the camera. Small smile, big sad eyes. That is the child from whom they will later take something away. She, who loved to live so terribly, is no longer allowed to participate. I want to push all the hurtful words anyone ever spoke to her back down their throats until they choke on them.

Words are harsh and merciless. I collect them in my head. Take away, received, gift, reward, guilt. I am looking for explanations on a daily basis, but I will never get a conclusive answer as to why this happened. I could bring in God, the Universe, or Fate. But so far, they're all just fairytales and sops. Stories to keep those who are left behind from drowning in the horror of ignorance.

On my timeline I have a period before, during, and after Julian. The central part has a sun, so bright it burns your eyes. Still, I want to look at it, from the darkness. I see her sitting in our old office. Surrounded by the art books and manuals that inspired her. For the umpteenth time I think about the many differences there were between us, but how we fit together like puzzle pieces. Like that time in Spain, both of us working at a large desk. I saw my glass of water move but thought I was mistaken. A few minutes later I felt a jolt, as if someone had moved my chair a bit. I opened my mouth to tell her that I'd had a supernatural experience, while she had already searched the Internet to find out if an earthquake had taken place in Frigiliana. Which, of course, was the case. She was wearing a striped t-shirt. She looked so young, so tanned, and so vital. So beautiful. Next to her computer was her framed vision board. Photos of everything she still wanted from life. Mine took up an entire wall in our office, hers fit into a ten-by-twenty-centimetre rectangle. A sea view with palm trees, a nice house, a music studio, a drum kit, the first cover of our magazine, and a photo of me. 'I've got almost everything I've ever wanted,' I still hear her say. She worked on *Et Alors,* listening to Gwen Stefani, Pharrell Williams, Justin Timberlake, and Gorillaz. When she took a break, she watched videoclips of Jimmy Fallon and Carpool Karaoke with James Corden. If she had been sitting for too long, she would dance. And I made her movements sync with the voice of Maria Callas on my headphones.

I'm looking for details. Everything was crystal clear while she was still alive, but now I fear I may have missed something. The time between the diagnosis and the day she died seems to dwarf everything. Those six long, dark, weeks seemed to act as a filter between me and the seven happy years. She was so much more than that sweet, helpless child she morphed into. But, every beautiful memory gets quickly pushed away by the image of death. Like a jammed slide projector that keeps returning, again and again, to the last picture.

=

American poet, and Pulitzer Prize winner, Mary Oliver mostly wrote about her love of the outdoors. She described the seasons, the blossom and the weeds, and the animals. Her disdain of human qualities like greed, and predatory exploitation, were often brought up, as well.

About her meeting with photographer Molly Malone Cook, at the home of Edna St. Vincent Millay, she wrote: 'I took one look and fell, hook and tumble. M. took one look at me, and put on her dark glasses, along with an obvious dose of reserve. She denied this to her dying day, but it was true.'

Oliver was twenty-four when they met, Cook thirty-four. The couple remained together for over 40 years and lived in Provincetown.

Oliver published more than fifteen collections of poetry and essays. Cook was one of the first photographers of *The Village Voice* and opened the East End Bookshop, where Norman Mailer regularly dropped in and where filmmaker John Waters could be found behind the register.

When Cook died in 2005, Oliver spent more than a year sorting out the thousands of photos and negatives her wife had left behind. Published in 2009, *Our World* is an intimate testament to their togetherness. Part memoir, part eulogy, it's a portrait of their shared love for life and their view of the world. In her poem 'When Death Comes,' Oliver wrote, 'When it's over, I want to say: all my life I was a bride married to amazement. I was the bridegroom, taking the world into my arms.'

=

My wife was not the easiest person to get to know. She was incredibly sweet, but to experience that side you first had to get through a few protective layers. Unless she trusted you instantly. Then, she would be by your side forever. She had some unwavering values. For the most part, they were about authenticity and she applied them to herself as well as to others. It could make her appear quite severe at times. If you knew her, she was empathetic, funny, articulate, and in possession of a sixth sense for other people's sorrow. She was good at analysing problems and, when asked, would give her opinion at length. That opinion could be harsh, and it sometimes took courage to hear it. She wasn't easy on herself, either. For years, a note hung on our refrigerator: 'An event is. You're the one who gives it a positive or negative value judgement.' We were heedful of the stories we told ourselves. My wife had a hard time dealing with people who were inconsistent, who talked a lot and did little. She also couldn't stand superficiality, and once in a while she'd put on her black sunglasses when in company she didn't like. Although I laughed inwardly, I told her I thought it was arrogant. She brushed it aside.

If I taught her anything, it was by holding a mirror up to her. I was able to show her that she was so much more than she knew. Because she always underestimated herself.

Sometimes she made bets with herself. If she could peel that apple in one slice, then the weather would be nice. If the light turned green before she got there, it would be a good day.

She loved music and sailing. Good food made her happy, she could spend hours in a pool, and she constantly learned new things. Ill-fitting clothes annoyed her, and she became irritable when she was hungry or when things got too busy. We had the same toddler humour, as she called it. In *On Writing*, Stephen King talks about his childhood and his babysitter's farts: 'It was as if I got a load of swamp-gas fireworks.' She spent almost a full day laughing about this. She was also convinced that Nicci French was not a duo and that Nicci Gerard alone wrote the books. Her husband was just there for show.

'How do you know?' I asked her.

'Well, how does one know something like that?'

Julian made me listen, not just with my rational mind but also with my intuition. One of the best gifts she has given me is confidence. She said that my ideas did not have to be confined within four walls, and made me aware of what I could be and become. We saw through each other and knew what the other needed and was capable of, even better than we knew ourselves. I was never quite able to cope with reality and she helped me maintain my fairytale world.

From the moment we got to know each other, she decided to build a new world with me, around us. I had someone next to me who believed in me to the deepest core of her being. I never wanted anyone else, and I wanted so badly to see her grow, to see her transform, and to witness who she would eventually become.

'Don't make me into a saint,' she said when she was dying.

Too late.

THE SURGERY HAD BEEN SUCCESSFUL, BUT OUR INITIAL JOY was ruined by the news that she still had to undergo two years of chemo and five years of hormone therapy. She asked the doctor whether he had any demonstrable reason for this. He didn't. It was 'just in case,' because you never knew if any cancer cells had escaped. My heart sank a few inches lower.

'Chemo weakens your immune system, making you more susceptible to cancer cells. So, wouldn't it make more sense to boost the immune system?' my wife wondered aloud. In theory, yes. But it usually doesn't work that way, we were told. So, that didn't get us any further.

To the doctor's surprise, Julian said she wanted to think about it. We would return the following week to discuss everything. As we left the doctor's office with shoulders slumped, we saw the other people sitting in the waiting room. Most of them bald or with a headscarf, sick and despondent.

'I don't want this,' said Julian. 'This is a black hole I'll never get out of.'

If she had already read tons of books when she was first diagnosed, that number was now being doubled. She read about chemotherapy as well as alternative therapies, and after a full week of reading and comparing, day and night, she was firmly convinced that she didn't want the treatment. That she must no longer eat animal protein. No more sugar either, because cancer cells are known to feed on it. And she'd need vitamin supplements to regain her strength. She asked me if I'd be on board with her not following the beaten path. In fact, she simply did what I myself would have done, and so I joined in with the diet. To make it as easy as possible for her. I knew it would be taxing to deviate from the standard treatment, and that she would be largely on her own with her worries and concerns. The day she told the doctor she would be opting for an alternative treatment only confirmed my suspicions about his disapproval. He, together with a nurse, aggressively questioned her, asked if she had any idea what she was doing, and said they would wash their hands of her if she didn't do what they prescribed. When she relayed to them how she had come to her decision, she was told she'd better leave the reading to the people who had studied the topic. There was no room for discussion. Julian had just undergone a double breast amputation, suffered a mental blow, and now she was on her own.

We left the hospital quite shaken. I felt sorry for my brave wife who, despite her firm beliefs, was obviously afraid. But she had me, and if I went for something I never gave up. I said we would make her better together. And, I was going to be the best vegan chef there ever was.

Julian would be worried for the rest of her life. Worried

that the cancer would return, that she had made the wrong choice. But, as the months passed and her body grew stronger, she gained a little more confidence. We were amazed at how difficult it was to find the right people outside of conventional medicine, but via our friends Peter and Luc we found an orthomolecular doctor with whom she felt comfortable and who treated her. Other than that, we were left to our own devices. But, we had hope and courage. Together we could take on the world.

=

What attracts me a lot about love and being in love is that, in part, you become someone else. Like a snake, you leave your old skin behind. You take the most essential parts with you, but something is added. In the best-case scenario, it makes you a better person. Previous boyfriends had called me tough, cold. One of them used the word 'ice queen.' I accused him of being overdramatic. Julian called me sweet, gentle, and exciting. I grew into the shape she assigned me. Pushed my arms and legs through the right holes, and stretched my back until it fit perfectly.

What would my former self have done, my current self wonders. I'd probably have drunk myself into total depression, and imagined I'd made up my wife's death in a delusion. Because finding the love of your life, and losing her at age 40, cannot possibly be real.

Alcohol reduces anxiety and tension by activating dopamine and serotonin receptors in the neural pathways of the pleasure centre. However, alcohol also disrupts neurobiological stress systems. Do we drink because we are depressed or do we get depressed because we drink? Even when the doctor suggests sleeping pills and antidepressants, I shake my head. I am not depressed. I am sad.

Before Julian and I left for Spain, we were enthusiastic partiers. Nights spent on the dance floor, gabbing in the pub or on a terrace after work. More than once, there were those mornings when we would 'never, never, never drink again' and yet were already sipping aperitifs by the evening. All that changed in Frigiliana. 'Our' village was four hundred metres above sea level and the hangovers turned out to be bottom-less. The altitude was Julian's explanation. Whatever the cause, one glass of wine led to a hangover that still lingered, four days later. Not being ones to give up easily, we tried everything. Different wine, different beer, bottled beer, draft beer, cocktails. You can't say we didn't try, but the headaches and listlessness ultimately forced us to give up drinking. I never started again, and I haven't drunk alcohol for over five years now. It has allowed me to focus more on creativity. To apply myself in a more focused and respectful way to what's important to me. Boy George told me the same thing in our conversation: 'Since I stopped drinking, my experiences are different than before. I love what I do and I enjoy being able to do it with a clear head.'

Even after Julian's death, I still don't allow external triggers into my body and life. I don't want anything to add to my grief, so no alcohol, no sugar, no pills, no negative people. There is no longer a barrier between life and my pain. No watered-down emotions. Only sharp edges. But they are *my* sharp edges.

*I learned how important it is to create
a framework in which fear doesn't
dominate your expression.*

In conversation with Quinn Delvaux
Et Alors? Magazine

I SAT ON THE BED, SWALLOWED, TRIED NOT TO GAG AND TO keep a straight face. In the hospital they had advised Julian to see a physiotherapist just a few days after the amputation. To prevent the scars from healing the wrong way. She, herself thought it was too early, but decided to do as she was told. She should have listened to herself, because after practising twice, her wound reopened. Out of a sense of duty, but with a lot of reluctance, I had peeked once before at what was underneath the large bandages: two large incisions, about six inches each. From under her armpits to the centre of her chest, with transverse stitches to hold it all together. Blue, yellow, and black skin discolorations with bumps and bulges that would hopefully disappear later. It was the most terrible mutilation I'd ever seen up close. What does it look like? she had asked. She wasn't ready to look at herself in the mirror. 'Challenging,' I'd said. However, it was going to become even more 'challenging' because, when the wound opened up again, there was a fissure in the centre of her left incision. I almost hit the floor when, at the clinic, they inserted a tube to see how deep it was inside. Almost one centimetre.

Wound care by a nurse twice a week, and on the other days I was allowed to do it.

'Beg your pardon?' I asked.

'Yes,' they said. 'It needs disinfecting and fresh dressings every day.'

I can't stand blood and almost pass out when I cut my finger. Now, here I was cleaning my wife's open wound. 'I can do this. I can do this. I can do this. I can do this,' I would tell myself beforehand. Julian lay on her back on the bed and looked at me. I was busy disinfecting my hands and preparing all the paraphernalia. I didn't want her to see that I was feeling sick and so I took a deep breath, as discreetly as possible.

'You probably didn't expect this when we got married,' she said.

'I'll do anything for you. You know that.'

'But there's no need for you to do this. We could also go to the nurse every day.'

'I can handle this,' I said boldly.

'You can handle anything; that doesn't mean you have to want to do it.'

A week later, I put on my white dress for effect and, like an accomplished caregiver, I removed the dressings, disinfected, washed, applied ointments and neatly covered everything up again.

'If you ever need a job ...' said the nurse. I drew my boundaries. It doesn't mean you have to want to do it.

=

Three months after her death, I get a stomachache. I lie down, waiting for it to stop. It doesn't. Two hours later, I'm crawling on my hands and knees towards my phone on the other side of the room. I hang slumped in the taxi that takes me to the nearest hospital. Once in the emergency room, I am wheeled under a scanner and painkillers are injected into my arm. I lie on my back on the gurney and almost suffocate in my tears. I don't know if they are from pain or from despair.

My digestive system appears to have ground to a halt. The doctors recognise me, and have read my story in the newspaper.
'She literally can't digest it,' I hear someone say.
'Count back from ten,' says someone else, pushing an anaesthetic mask over my mouth. It is him who is standing next to me when I wake up hours later. He takes my hand and says sorry. Says he couldn't possibly do that. I look at him inquisitively. Apparently, I had asked him to make a mistake while putting me to sleep. I can't remember.
I look away and start to cry again. 'Be careful, crying,' he says. 'You mustn't use your abs for a few weeks.'

After a few days I'm allowed to go home, and I spend hours in the bathtub. No one has told me that grieving is so painful. And so physically, too. I read about holes in hearts. About prolapsing stomachs and nausea. I have none of that. I have shoulders that are level with my ears and, in the morning, it takes me hours before I can walk more or less normally. Every part is straining, working against me, and I have a constant muscle spasm. If she were here, she would have kissed my stomach. She would have said the scars were going to make me even more beautiful. She would have been outraged at the nurse who left a black-and-blue bruise where the IV had been.

Her bones were becoming brittle. From now on she could break, the doctor had said one week before her death. I think that's when my body started to protest.

OUR RELATIONSHIP SHIFTED AFTER THE OPERATION. EARLIER, it was she who'd stop me when I stepped out in front of a car daydreaming, or grab me by the scruff of my neck when I almost fell down a manhole. Keeping you in one piece is a full-time job, she often said.

After her operation, I was the one who protected her. On the street I walked between her and other people. In a crowd I stood in front of her, even though she was much taller than me. She took it in her stride, which was not her habit. I wanted to give her time to figure out how to deal with this altered body. The Julian before the operation would have found my mothering oppressive. Not so, the one after, and sometimes she'd lean heavily against me in public. I would put an arm round her and say it was okay.

'I'm maimed,' she would say. 'A victim of botched surgery,' she sometimes said.

When the wounds started to heal, the swelling subsided and the bruises disappeared, I said it looked fine. She still didn't want to look in the mirror.

'How can you still find me beautiful?' she wondered aloud.

'I think you are the most beautiful person there is.' I noticed she didn't believe me.

When she got out of the shower, I often took off my shirt and gently stood up against her. My intact breasts against her scars. She needed to know that I didn't shy away from anything.

=

Until three years ago I was having nightmares. There was a man standing next to my bed, completely hidden in the shadows, with no clear outline. His head was a bird cage. Every nightmare made me wake up screaming. Something that's still shudderingly affirmed by all who have ever lain next to me. In my dream I would open my eyes, see him and scream myself awake. I've had this nightmare for as long as I can remember. I was about three years old when it started. My mother showed me Magritte's painting, but that was nowhere near what it looked like.

'Just listen to what I'm reading now!' Julian was in an Elizabeth Gilbert phase and after the beautiful *The Signature of All Things* she had started on *Eat, Pray, Love*. Gilbert had told her medicine man in Bali that she regularly had nightmares in which she saw a man with a knife standing next to her bed. The medicine man told her that the Balinese believe that, in the womb, we are accompanied by four brothers. They represent intelligence, friendship, strength, and poetry. They come into the world with us, are our protectors, and keep us safe and happy. After death you will be picked up by your four brothers and taken to heaven. He said she had been misinterpreting her dream for years. That the man was her brother and was not there to attack her, but to protect her.

Could it be that simple, I thought? Whatever it was, forty-one years of nightmares came to an end after she read me a scene from a book. That's what she did for me.

*I get the feeling that people are way
more focused now on creating,
expressing their freedom and
celebrating who they are. It's almost like
a statement.*

In conversation with Jorge Clar
Et Alors? Magazine

I REMEMBER HOW HAPPY WE WERE WHEN WE LEFT FOR SPAIN
after the operation. Back to our home on the mountain. We
had been staying in Antwerp for three months, but at home
she would get stronger, get back in shape, and we would get
on with our lives. On the outward journey, we had taken our
worries and tears to every petrol station and hotel on the
side of the road. Now we intuitively gave a wide berth to the
places where we had been, earlier.

We had to stop quite often. Julian could not sit in the
same position for long, and there was a time limit on the seat
belt pressure. Nevertheless, hope and relief are strong mo-
tivators, so it didn't matter a bit. In our minds, we were
cruising in a convertible with Massive Attack blaring from
the speakers. In reality we were driving our ancient car.
When we came to live in Spain, we had bought a Renault
Clio of indeterminate paleness for eight hundred euros. 'This
is the one,' she'd said in the used-car lot. And she'd put her
head on the roof. 'Hello, car.' I'd stared in astonishment,
from her to the car, which looked like someone had pelted

it with stones, and just shrugged.

'Fine,' I said, wiping the streak of dust from her cheek while laughing.

The salesman threw in a cassette tape of Julio Iglesias for free. Afterwards, the tape turned out to be stuck in the cassette player. A poisoned gift.

Amo la vida y amo el amor
Soy un truhán, soy un señor
Algo bohemio y soñador

Had our impatient anticipation been too great? Neither of us could put our finger on it, but our homecoming was disappointing.

'I no longer enjoy being here,' she said that same evening.

I had to agree.

The heavy scent of the jasmine blossom, which before I had found so intoxicating and magical, now felt suffocating. We no longer relished the sparkling blue sea or the spectacle of pink sunsets.

First, we looked for it within ourselves. We lived in a paradise. What was wrong with us for not being able to enjoy this? And worse, that it actually made us despondent? We suddenly needed more than this little house on the mountain. More culture, more exhibitions, more input than the village chatter about the thriving of avocados and oranges.

We had become aware of our own mortality, for sure. It had also become clear that life could, just like that, without asking permission, take a different direction. What we now realised was that it was impossible to proceed in the same way as before. We needed something big. Something as yet unknown. To overwrite the fear of her being ill. She, because she had to give space to her anxiety. I, because I had never thought that I could actually lose her.

'Give me three months,' she said, 'and I'll be in top form again.'

'Then we'll go to New York,' I added. 'That's vast. Inspiring and new.'

=

After her death, people cautiously say it would have been better if she had opted for chemotherapy. Then she would still be alive. I tell them it's just the opposite. The tumours in her head had been growing for ten years. Eight years earlier, they could have done something about it, but not after that. When she got breast cancer, they had missed the tumours in her head. If they'd seen them, she would never have left the hospital. Attempts would have been made to save her. According to the doctors I spoke with, there was no longer any chance of recovery, and this scenario was bound to play out, no matter what. If she had opted for chemo, we would never have had the last eighteen months. She would have remained ill until her death.

For the first time, ignorance was bliss. Julian fully embraced life and declined all follow-up treatments. This way she made it possible for us to carry out a project like 22, and we lived in oblivion for another year and a half.

Time and again, the story persuades me to believe in something bigger, and I hope to one day witness the effect that those last eighteen months of her life have had. Because, to believe that everything is a coincidence or that we just had bad luck would be an insult to the extraordinary life we have lived.

If you knew beforehand what would happen, would you make the same choices again? When I think about that immense, unconditional love, I know I would choose it again in the blink of an eye. Without a second's hesitation. Because, despite all that pain, I instinctively know that love is bigger than that. 'Don't forget to notice the collateral beauty,' I heard in a film recently. Don't forget to notice the collateral beauty. And, with it, all the ensuing reasons why I would never make a different choice.

AFTER HER REHABILITATION, WE BOOKED A FLIGHT TO NEW York. All the surgery and the turmoil had made us smaller. The city was bigger than us, and therefore perfect. I had never been there; Julian had only passed through. We had arranged a home swap through Home Exchange: we'd spend two months in New York while the owners of the beautiful loft apartment on Great Jones Street enjoyed our home in Spain. The lady of the house was a ballerina, and taught classes in the dance studio adjoining the bedroom. In the morning we'd take a run-up and slide across the polished floor towards the kitchen. In the evening, we exorcised the freezing cold that had seeped in our bodies during the day in the two-person tub. Julian was still a bit shaky, and although her wounds were healing well, she had limited energy. As soon as her eyelids drooped or she started to slow down a bit, I suggested we go home. Knowing she'd be horrified to limit me in what I wanted to do, I would claim to be tired.

After a day out in town she was exhausted, and we spent our evenings watching Gilmore Girls under a blanket on the couch, surrounded by healthy snacks bought at Whole Foods.

'How uncool can a person become?' she asked, laughing.

'So much more,' I said. And I put on a pair of Christmas socks.

On Christmas Eve we watched, intertwined, the snow through the window. Later we wrote down everything we didn't want to take into the New Year on a piece of paper and burned it out on our terrace. A ritual that we used to do each year with Renate. On mine I wrote 'sickness, worry, fear, panic.' Watching the snowflakes put out the fire, I realised she had probably written the same things.

During the day, the city was our playground, and we walked from one exhibition to another. We were blown away by Kara Walker, whose work revolves around African-American racial identity. We were happy that Carmen Herrera, despite her age, had been able to witness her retrospective at the Whitney, and Julian spent hours in front of Andreas Gursky's photographs. Kerry James Marshall's exhibit at The Met left us dazed with admiration. He uses paintings, collage, and video to explore the history of Black identity. To address the racial politics, emancipation, and cultural representation of Black people within art history, with its almost exclusively white faces. To 'fill the gap in the image bank' as he himself puts it. And at Hauser & Wirth, a security guard gave us a guided tour of the Paul McCarthy exhibition. Distorted variations of Disney's seven dwarfs, juxtaposed with the original clay statues and their moulds.

'I love fairytales,' the guard sighed. A man who was at least three feet taller and wider than me.

'Me too,' I sighed along with him.

'You're lucky,' he said to Julian. 'She looks like Ariel.'

Julian beamed at me.

'Yes, I am very lucky.'

=

At one of my lodgings, there are two cats looking after me. 'What did you do today?' I ask them after I've been out to do some shopping. I never used to care for pets, but suddenly I've fallen madly in love. Is it possible to acquire the traits of a loved one who is no longer there? Julian loved animals and children. If we ever settled down somewhere, she planned to get some cats and a dog. Or maybe two dogs, so they could play together. Dogs and cats looked straight into her eyes and stopped right in front of her until she bent down to pet them. They docilely placed their heads in her hand. Wash your hands first! I'd yell, disgusted by bacteria and disease, when she wanted to touch me afterwards. What a nag I was. Nevertheless, it continued to amaze me, as that connection was completely lacking in me. Babies locked eyes with her, and many a mother looked up in surprise when her child stopped crying; or smiled ear to ear. If there was a toddler on the plane, they could be found in the aisle next to her seat. Playing quietly. There was no talk. How did that happen, I wondered then, and still do. She herself did not want children, because she didn't want to give birth. But she would never deny her partner a desire to have children. She had decided on that at a young age. Later on, it just turned out to be impractical. Due to her work, and also because not a single girlfriend ever brought up the subject. Neither did I. Paradoxically, we had an ideal image of a large family. A big table, with children and friends, and her at the stove. We were very much aware that we had probably picked up that image from the countless films in which the cosiness of family life played a major role. It probably doesn't even exist, she said when she voiced her fantasy. If we ever settled down somewhere, we might be able to adopt. Not just one kid but many, like Jolie and Pitt in better times. Or, else, just a dog. Or two.

While I'm writing, one of the cats squeezes between the edge of the table and my tummy. He gently anchors his tiny claws into my thigh and falls asleep. As soon as dusk arrives, he meows until I move to the couch, so he can nestle into my lap. The second cat crawls under my arm and puts her paw on my chest. I balance my book in such a way as to not disturb their peace. Otherwise, they might leave. And the warmth feels good. I position my hand so I can feel their breath on my skin and I think about my wife's final weeks. How I sometimes held my face near her mouth when she slept and felt the down on my cheek stand up. How I lay close to her, breathing on her neck to make her feel that I was there. Because, putting my arm around her had become too heavy for her frail body.

When I have to leave the house for good, my heart takes a little leap and I decide not to rent a place with pets again. How much loss can there be on top of loss, before everything collapses?

It's not our intention to make radical work nor are we aiming for a revolution, rather we try to build a bridge, to have a dialogue with people who might not be very aware.

In conversation with The Transketeers
Et Alors? Magazine

IT WAS THE WORK OF OTHER PEOPLE THAT KEPT CHALLENGING us and made us ask questions. We admired artists who re-created reality, who addressed history. Every morning we woke up with new ideas and the necessity to turn them into reality. We had never been interested in creating things of beauty. Our work mainly needed to ask the right questions. If you want to understand a particular period in history, look at what the artists were doing. They are the visionaries, the ones who bring the oxygen to a society. Art gives people a broader view, so for us it was the perfect medium to try and change things.

Those weeks in New York, we talked late into the night about what we wanted to do with our lives. We dusted off our wedding project. We'd put the idea aside when she got sick, but now that she was better, anything was possible.

Julian and I were both convinced that optimism is most likely to generate change. Why point out every difference when you could connect just as well through recognition? Referring to a hopeful event, such as a marriage, would establish the recognition that is essential to furthering understanding. To marry for love. Even two women. Just like everyone else. 'Even if, through our performance, just a single person questions the fact that we can only marry in twenty-two countries,' she said, 'it's already meaningful.'

What if we go all out on this? What do we need and what do we leave behind; how much are we willing to sacrifice? And, what if it doesn't work? What's the worst-case scenario? What if we get rid of everything and our project doesn't work? And, what if it leaves us flat broke? So, we started budgeting. How much did we need per month? We ended up with food, transportation, and accommodation. If we no longer had any fixed monthly payments, we might make it, but it would mean giving up our house. But, was that so bad? Maybe we could sleep on someone's couch in every country. Travel was also a challenge, but we might be able to find sponsors for that. An airline, or the railways. We had some savings, and if we sold everything we owned, we would get by for some time. Julian created an ambitious Excel sheet with all the expenses and we concluded that we had enough money for five marriages. From the sixth one on, we would need those sponsors and that sofa bed. But, if our plan failed, we would lose everything in a heartbeat. Were we willing to risk it? Yes, we were, we told each other with a brave face. To be honest, there was a tinge of panic in our voices. But our enthusiasm was greater.

We got out pen and paper and made lists of everything we needed to start the project. From finding an official who wanted to marry us symbolically, to a plane ticket, a wedding dress and suit, a camera, potential sponsors, a photographer; everything was written down. My wife let loose and, as our to-do list took shape, our imaginations began to work overtime.

We wanted to have wedding photos taken at every ceremony to maybe display them afterwards. And could we also make a documentary? And, what we mustn't forget was that we also wanted to interview people who had helped make same-sex marriage legal in their own country. We intended to subsequently publish those interviews in *Et Alors?* to complete the circle.

'How many lives do we have now?' My wife asked, laughing.

'Ah,' I replied, 'We can do it!'

It was New Year's Day 2017, we had laid the groundwork for 22 and were watching the sun rise. Tired from our nocturnal planning, I stood in front of the window, looking out at the snow and the early-morning walkers. Kitty-corner from us, the Great Jones Street fire station. A Santa Claus and a Christmas tree above the gate. Lights everywhere, even in the blue-grey morning glow. The set of a Tim Burton movie.

Cold feet. She wrapped a blanket around me and took me in her arms. I leaned against her. Feeling safe. Warm.

'Do you know how much I love you?' she asked.

'How much?'

'If you take off from here to the nearest star and then you go from one star to another until you've visited them all then you circle the earth a few more times before coming back here. That distance is how much I love you.'

'That much?' I asked.

'That much.'

=

Drawings of hypermasculine men on motorcycles, in leather suits and lumberjack shirts. All with gigantic erect penises. Black men, white men, policemen and sailors, copulating in parks and prisons.

In a country where homosexuality could lead to imprisonment, hospitalisation, castration, or a lobotomy, Touko Laaksonen from Finland made his illustrations just for himself, for most of his life. In 1957 he sent his drawings to the American Physique Pictorial. His style differed totally from the post-WWII images, which usually depicted gay men as feminine and ultra-sensitive. It explained his popularity in the gay subcultures of the 1950s. By 1970 he was publishing erotic comic strips and had made his entry into the art world. In 1973 he resigned from McCann-Erickson in Helsinki, to work full time on his drawings. Touko's partner, Veli 'Nipa' Mäkinen, known to his family as 'the room-mate,' died in 1981. They had been together for twenty-eight years. After his partner's death, Laaksonen said: 'In the ten years since Veli passed away, he has never really left me. Every now and then I hear him stumbling clumsily around the house, as he always did. Sometimes I feel someone close to me, and I know it is him. Most of the time I find his presence very comforting, but sometimes when I'm trying to draw, he suddenly blows or whistles in my ear. Infuriating me with it, just as much as when he was alive.'

With more than 3,500 illustrations which span 40 years, he has been called the 'most influential' designer of gay pornographic images. In 1971, the ban on sex between two men or women was lifted in Finland, and Touko Laaksonen, too, could now publicly identify himself as 'Tom of Finland' in his own country.

=

In the mirror I see an old woman who resembles me. When Julian and I were together, I never felt like I was getting older. And, I myself still saw her as the woman I had first laid eyes on seven years earlier. Now that she's gone, I wonder when those years were added. In *Totality and Infinity* Levinas writes that the face reflects the idea of infinity. 'It is not you who gives the world a place, but it is the Other who speaks to you, appeals to you and gives you a place.' If Western philosophy starts from the 'I,' Levinas turns the tables and says that it's the other who makes you responsible. Only when someone else looks at one and appeals to one, does one become an 'I,' a someone. The other, as a condition for one's existence. In his *The Phenomenology of Spirit*, Hegel also talks about how human consciousness is formed through a struggle for mutual recognition with the other. That in the other lies our self-consciousness. It reminds me of Jeff Koons' reflective surfaces, through which he seeks to affirm the viewer.

If a tree falls in a forest and no one is around to hear it, does it make a sound?

It's a well-known question, and George Berkeley answers it with: 'The objects of sense exist only when they are perceived; the trees therefore are in the garden ... no longer than while there is somebody by to perceive them.' When the trees are not seen, they do not exist. When there are no ears to hear it, there is no sound.

In quantum mechanics one speaks of the 'observer effect.' A quantum potentiality only manifests itself, or only becomes physical, when someone looks at it. Can something exist without being perceived? Who am I, now that Julian is no longer watching, I wonder? Suddenly, I am seven years older than when I was with her. Her constant gaze made time stand still.

The weather has become warmer, but I can't feel it. People walk around with bare arms and pallid legs. I feel cold, and am unable to absorb the heat. I'm trying to function as best as I can, but the life around me remains a picture projected on the glass walls of the bell jar, which I am trapped under, and I stare in disbelief at the life that just keeps going on around me. There is a new me in the making. She is wary, and not sure yet if she wants to be here. Whether she's going to stay or not.

'You'd be even more beautiful if you smiled,' says a man who passes me on the street. He looks at me and winks. I thought I had been dusted with a layer of grief, but apparently that's not the case. The man is lying. This morning I was despondently looking in the mirror. I couldn't find the energy to get rid of the dark circles under my eyes. I haven't used make-up since the day Julian was admitted to hospital.

My face is blank. When I go out to eat, I sit with my back to the people in the restaurant. There is no filter between me and the rest of the world. My nerves are exposed on the surface, and I am too naked to be viewed head-on.

'People who have recently lost someone have a certain look, recognizable maybe only to those who have seen that look on their own faces. I have noticed it on my face and I notice it now on others. The look is one of extreme vulnerability, nakedness, openness. It is the look of someone who walks from the ophthalmologist's office into the bright daylight with dilated eyes, or of someone who wears glasses and is suddenly made to take them off,' Joan Didion writes. But when you are grieving, you also lack the energy to look any different than that.

I'm amazed at my hair. It's almost obscene how healthy and shiny it remains. My hair is not mourning with me. One day the phone rings, when I'm standing in front of the mirror with a pair of scissors. There's no one on the other end of the line. I hang up and put the scissors back in the drawer.

You'd be even more beautiful if you smiled.

I'll be happy if I can ever smile again. So I think. And, I keep walking.

Ten minutes later, I hit the ground. Suddenly, without stumbling. One minute I am walking, the next I feel my face scraping against the concrete. A woman presses a tissue to my mouth. Red. She asks if I'm okay. My shoulder is bruised, my knee is swollen, and my face is lacerated.

'It's post-traumatic stress,' says the doctor who stitches up my lip. 'What you've been through has caused a trauma that may stress you out for years, if not forever.' I must also watch out for 'complicated grief': inheriting the symptoms of your loved one's illness. Something my body has done before, when my digestion came to a halt.

When I get home, I read some more: A 2013 study from the *Journal of Public Health* shows that there is a 66 percent chance of a widow dying within three months of the death of her partner. Previous studies mentioned 90 percent. It's referred to as the 'widowhood effect.' Doctors claim not to know why the mortality rate is so high, and attribute it to increased stress and neglect of the widow's health. Nobody talks about a broken heart.

I read that the grieving process is easier if you've been able to say goodbye. However, nothing prepared me for the trauma I suffered after watching the love of my life deteriorate and die. My body protests, as if it were switching itself off. I regularly cry so hard it makes me throw up. And, now the outside is also messed up. When I feel a crying fit coming on, I have to keep a straight face. Otherwise, my upper lip will split open again. I look in the mirror. At my damaged face and my stooped gait. This is the person I'll have to deal with from now on. I am in pain, and feel humiliated. Humiliated by the flood of negativity. When am I allowed to start feeling sorry for myself?

I crawl into bed. It's four in the afternoon. Enough is enough. I am alone. She would have kissed me better.

Being queer is about remembering the radical roots of the gay liberation movement, and acknowledging that change doesn't usually come without a fight and that fighting doesn't always look the same for everyone.

In conversation with With JJ Levine
Et Alors? Magazine

OUR STAY IN NEW YORK CAME TO AN END AND WE FLEW BACK home. Full of excitement to start the preparations for 22. And our new life. Our plan was to finalise all practical matters in Spain, and then travel back to New York on a three-month tourist visa for the production of the project. At the end of our stay, we would get married for the first time, and then continue our travels. Once again, we got rid of all our things, and it was amazing how much we had accumulated in the last three years. Clothes, piles of books and little knick-knacks like vintage ashtrays (although we didn't smoke), and pretty wine glasses (although we didn't drink). For the second time, we promised to never, ever, buy anything again.

Our emigration to Spain had been exciting. But, at that time we still had the prospect of a home, and of stability. Now, we were stepping onto a tightrope that connected our present with our future. Not at all sure if it would last.

Julian tacked large sheets of paper to our office wall and drew up a schedule counting down to our departure date and listing everything we needed to take care of before then. From a dental check-up, to contacting the used-furniture shop a few villages down the road. It felt wonderful, this slow countdown to nothing, which would allow us to then build up again.

Next to the paper sheets she created a vision board. Wedding dresses she liked, a GoPro camera, places she wanted to visit in all the countries where we were getting married. But, also, everything that inspired her. In New York, we had met my favourite writer, Siri Hustvedt. She had signed her latest book to me with: 'Don't forget to look at those inner pictures,' because during our conversation we'd talked about the many ideas that were projected into my head, like photographs. Afterwards, Julian read everything by Hustvedt and put a copy of her words up on the wall. As a reminder, she said.

To detach from the world, that is to say, to no longer have a home and a base, is harder than expected, and time and again we had to explain what we were about to do. Our plan had elicited a lot of enthusiasm and support, but that didn't make it any easier. We ended up having to register at my mother's address because the government required a postal address for tax purposes. You couldn't just disappear, and even travelling the world came with its obligations. After all the tasks - big and small - on our wall had been ticked off, we booked our ticket, and put all our household goods by the front door with a sign saying: FREE. By the evening everything was gone, and we had to borrow glasses and some plates from the neighbours. In our enthusiasm we had forgotten that we ourselves needed something to eat off for a few more days.

We would be taking one suitcase each. Only black clothes, we decided. That's what we wore most, and it's practical on the road. Everything can be washed together. As for the rest: two MacBooks, two Kindles, a camera, and a tripod. I had a pair of high-heeled shoes and ballet flats. She: 'smart' shoes and All Stars. The notebooks with all our plans, and the chargers for our electricals, ensured that everything filled up quickly. I looked at the two suitcases with some consternation.

'So, this is it.' Disconcerted that this was all that was left after forty-two years of being alive.

'It's just stuff,' she said. She kissed me on the head and closed the suitcases. A few minutes later, we dropped our house keys in Scott's mailbox and got the bus down our mountain, to the airport.

=

When she was dying, I asked her if she had had a good life. She said that I had made her very happy, but it had been far too short. That she wanted to do so much more. Wanted us to be together so much longer. That it was not enough.

Henry Thoreau retreated to the woods to search for the essence of life. To forestall discovering, on his deathbed, that he had not lived. Julian had lived. But not enough. Now I want her to be proud of me. But, how did she want me to carry on? Am I required to enjoy my life one hundred per cent, because she no longer has that option? I must go in search of my Walden Pond. Of my essence. Maybe I shouldn't put so much pressure on myself.

The only way to be happy is to acknowledge mortality, because then life becomes valuable. As Audre Lorde wrote in *The Cancer Journals*: 'Once I accept the existence of dying as a life process, who can ever have power over me again?'

I watched Julian decline. My wife died in my arms. What could possibly still have power over me? Belief in a self-fulfilling prophecy prevents me from saying that nothing worse could happen to me. Bad plus bad is worse, and is always possible. But, it no longer holds any power over me. I do fear that the pain and sorrow will never go away, but I no longer fear death, and shrug it off. I don't like this apathy.

Historically there has been limited gay imagery in mainstream art because it has not been a socially accepted expression. But I'm ever hopeful that that is changing.

Michael Schreiber On Bernard Perlin
Et Alors? Magazine

ARRIVING IN NEW YORK FOR THE SECOND TIME, WE WERE cooking pasta in the kitchen at 4:00 a.m. Julian had read that the best way to prevent jet lag was to fast during the flight. Eager, as always, we had embraced this idea. Looking a bit pale around the gills, we had been encouraging each other for ten hours, taking sips of water now and then. It was June, and very hot. I was reading Paul Auster's *4321* and felt his description of the bricks 'oozing with sweat' in my core. The jet lag lasted two days, and we only got out of bed to shower and open the door for the person delivering our Indian takeaway. We listened to the neighbour's chatter and knew we were in the right place. A good start to our new adventure.

'I could live this way,' said Julian. 'With you, in bed, with a stack of books and magazines. And eating curry every day.'

We chose New York for the first wedding because it's where we felt most at home. Here we had conversations with strangers on the subway, and even I was able to find my way around. Julian always seemed to have a built-in GPS, while I could get lost in a metre square. Not in New York. Everything went so fast, and I could wholeheartedly say 'wow' and 'amazing' and 'awesome.' I could be brazenly ambitious here. According to Julian, on the European continent every form of ambition had been nipped in the bud by its grand history. An unfair competition, in which the puny individual always loses out to the worship of saints, and the origin stories tied round our necks like nooses, leaving deep marks as soon as one desires more. Any aspiration is seen as megalomania, and she couldn't keep track of how many times she'd been told *Doe maar gewoon*[1] at school.

Once in New York, we talked a lot about our performance and our hopes to generate more awareness as a result. People said 'wow' and 'amazing' and 'awesome' and we believed we were going to change the world.

=

No clairvoyants, she'd said in a lucid moment, weeks before she died. I laughed. She knew my fondness for everything magical. In New York I made a habit of photographing every table and window where a fortune teller was advertising their skills. A fondness kept at a distance, because I was too super-stitious to actually go inside. I believe that knowing things you shouldn't know brings bad luck. The only 'knowledge' I didn't wish to acquire. Not then. Fortunately.

1   The complete expression, *Doe maar gewoon, dat is al gek genoeg* (literally, Just act normal, that's crazy enough.) is used to discourage people from 'showing off,' including from visibly excelling at something.

People say that our love is endless and that she's still with me. Those are empty words and lazy conclusions. They hurt me, even though they are well-meaning. I look for her in every room I enter, in all the faces I see, and in every mirror I pass. Oftentimes I sit down and tell myself to feel. I really must feel. Because, if she's there, I have to let her in. I feel nothing.

During the crying spells, which are still so intense that I sometimes fear I'll remain stuck, I beg her for a sign. A sign that she is doing alright. That she's not somewhere cold and dark. That my bleak fantasy is not true. But I don't get a sign. Not even a little one. And I have to conclude that dead means dead. That a soul may weigh 21 grams, but that doesn't mean that it stays with us. And, I hope that soon everyone will stop saying things that only serve to reassure themselves. I go to bed alone; I get up alone and I walk through the city without her. She's not there when I turn to speak to her in an unguarded moment.

Friends do make me waver when they tell me about consulting a psychic, and the healing experience it brought them. No harm in trying, right? Obviously, I feel guilty, since she'd told me not to do this, but in my mind I tell her it's okay. However, if I consult this psychic, shouldn't I believe that Julian already knows this? That there's no need to tell her? I think it's all very complicated.

In the lift to the apartment, I feel terribly nervous. Inside, I am warmly welcomed with tea and biscuits. When I have taken a seat, the psychic puts on some music and proceeds to seek contact. After a while he tells me that Julian lived by the water, that she did boating. He mentions ceremonies that would have taken place at this time. These are all things that were in the newspapers. I want something that surprises me, that makes me believe.

Then he says that we had locked ourselves in for a while. I sit up a little straighter. Our seclusion in Spain lasted three years. He says I barely go out. That I'm alone too much. And that this is not a good idea. 'Spring is coming. And Julian says you're too beautiful to lock yourself up,' he says.

He tells me that I always gave her that little push she needed. That I was the only one to ever see what she was capable of. That I had made her very strong, but that I now have to be just as strong for myself. He also says she's still holding my hand. And that she will continue to do so for the rest of my life. That we had and still have our own language. That I have to watch for signs.

'Is she okay?' I ask, crying. It's all I want to know.

'Yes,' he says. 'She's okay.'

I go home, confused and not knowing how to believe what I want to believe so badly.

'My love,' I write in a letter that evening. 'Was that you?'

Collage is about combining different kinds of images to explain a feeling or a mood. My work reflects the exuberant world I would like to live in.

In conversation with Agustín Martínez
Et Alors? Magazine

FOR HOURS ON END, WE WALKED ALL OVER THE CITY MAKING plans for 22. Once we had prepared our dossier and finalised our budget, our days consisted of sending emails, running in and out of meetings, and making Skype calls to Europe in the middle of the night, because of the time difference.

It soon became clear that our project entailed a logistical challenge and could not be easily organised remotely and online. Although we had five people proofread our application form for clarity, Kafka was still omnipresent. I can't remember how many times I had to explain that it was a symbolic – and not an official – marriage, because otherwise we'd have to get divorced each time. That would've taken the romance out of it, big time. And, that all we needed was one official, who was authorised to perform a wedding ceremony, in an official place and in front of the camera. People thought we were weird, and we knew it would get easier after the first wedding. Then we'd have a concrete example. But, we needed to plan far in advance. Since we had no home to return to in between, everything had to flow together seamlessly. Every country, every overnight stay, and every flight or train journey had to be consecutive, and every extra day was at the expense of our budget.

How much organisation is required to make this happen, one might ask. A lot, it turned out, because it's a situation that doesn't follow standard procedures. Consequently, most people have no idea how to handle this. In some cities we were sent from pillar to post in such an exasperating manner that I ended up writing to say it was no longer necessary. That we would pick another place. After all, it was the country that mattered, not the city. Miraculously, those were the magic words. On closer inspection, no major city wanted to hand over the project at that point. Once the city was settled, the official paperwork followed, because even a symbolic marriage requires hundreds of signatures.

Simultaneously, the search was on for sponsors. A laundry list of possible brands that were vetted for their stance on LGBTQ+ issues, and then contacted if found to be correct. From clothing companies, to hospitality, to transportation.

We had enough money for five marriages and had previously discussed whether we should wait until we had the entire budget covered. But, no, that was not an option. We would go full throttle and see how things turned out. Do what we always did. Somehow, it always worked out. Undeniably, there was some stress. A whole lot of stress, even. Can we afford all this? What if it doesn't work, then we are literally penniless. Moreover, Julian's surgery had brought her a lot of feelings of insecurity. She tried hard not to yield to worry, but sometimes it flared up viciously. 'I see you,' I said regularly, trying to reassure her. I think it helped.

People told us how fearless and brave we were. We always thought they were talking about someone else, and looked over our shoulders like cartoon characters. But, we had each other, and we made each other brave, and we said that postponing would never accomplish anything and that security was an expensive illusion. The latter was printed on the tag of a Yogi teabag.

=

I look at all the work we have created over the years. Series like *Clark Kent*, a group of collages in which Julian and I, seen from the back, are looking at various billboards at pictures of families advertising vacations. A man and a woman, embracing closely, in the name of a clothing brand. Father, mother, and two children drinking coke on a bus decorated with Christmas baubles.

We created the series from our daily reflections on what we're seeing when we look around us. A society filled with collective family aspirations and heteronormative images. Where gays in advertising remain a rarity, and are even considered offensive by some people. We wondered how identity is formed when you don't have any visible role models. When you don't see anything around you that you can identify with. The title comes from one of my favourite movie monologues. In Quentin Tarantino's *Kill Bill*, David Carradine talks about Superman. How he gets up in the morning as Superman and disguises himself as Clark Kent to move among people. His glasses and suit are his costume, while the cape with the big red S is his normal outfit. You become what you surround yourself with, as the saying goes.

Actually, I'm still doing what I most loved to do as a child: cutting, pasting, and writing stories about what I had cut and pasted. Usually, I sat at the kitchen table, or any table, depending on the house where we happened to live. A stack of magazines, scissors, a bottle of Pritt, paper, a pack of marker pens, and a lot of imaginary friends. Sometimes, my mother would give me bits of leftover wool. If I cut them or tried to glue them, they would fray and get stuck to my fingers or in my hair. I looked at the world around me and tried out the different perspectives on paper. Series: a sequence of images or actions on the same theme. Still my favourite form of understanding. Repeating. Grouping. Arranging. The same set of motifs in different configurations.

In his essay *Mourning and Melancholia*, Freud talks about this grouping. The serial development through different representations of the same thing. He calls this *Trauerarbeit*, 'the work of mourning.' Necessary, because the reference point upon which all your love was focused has disappeared. He suggests that there is nothing natural about grieving, that your brain automatically resists any activity that causes pain. What do we do with all the thoughts about the deceased, but also: how do we treat those thoughts? By repeating. Grouping. Arranging. Viewing everything from different angles.

In *The New Black,* psychoanalyst Darian Leader compares it to Cubism. A fragmentary composition of an image, viewed from different perspectives. He continues the line to De Chirico and Morandi. The same set of motifs, repeated over and over again, in different configurations. 'We tend to repeat things when we are stuck in them,' he says.

Any attempt to place my work in a narrative framework ends in mourning, and because I'm unable to reduce Julian to just one story, I create several. Each one from a different angle. I am writing a book. I'm working on a documentary. I'm sorting her photographs in preparation for a new series. My wife as a collage. As a whole consisting of many parts. In an effort to understand this situation.

After the publication of *Before Forgetting*, a novel about the death of his mother, Peter Verhelst said in an interview: 'I didn't lick my wounds, I gave them shape. Because shaped grief is more manageable than formless grief.' The work of mourning.

I aim to contradict the notion that, in order to change one's sex, one must undergo major surgery and commit to a lifetime of supplemental hormones.

In conversation with Heather Cassils
Et Alors? Magazine

I PROUDLY SHOWED OFF OUR APPROVED MARRIAGE application for the photo. Every moment was captured. The first marriage for 22 was the only one that was performed legally, and not just symbolically. In New York you can get married as often as you want. Even though you are already married. With the same person, that is. We thought it was an exciting idea, an American marriage certificate. However, organising the wedding wasn't as straightforward as all that. The city strives to marry as many people as possible, so the wedding ceremony only lasts a minute, the so-called New York Minute. And, so, there was no time for performances or to set up our camera. We did not let ourselves get discouraged, and the next day we sought out the kindest-looking official. We had to let twelve couples go in front of us, but at last his window was available. After I relayed the whole story, he laughed out loud. 'This is so weird, you girls are so weird!' he said, laughing. But also: 'This is amazing!' And the latter secured us an appointment with Michael McSweeney, the New York City Clerk.

McSweeney thought 22 was so special that he decided to marry us personally. A great honour. 'But what about that New York Minute?' I asked him. 'In New York, we walk fast, we eat fast, we drink fast, and we work fast. And we get married fast, because we have to walk, eat, drink and work fast,' he said with rehearsed speed. I looked at him wide-eyed. But, especially for us, and for our great project, he decided to go for the 'full option.' A full three minutes.

After this conversation, we lingered on the steps of the Marriage Bureau, looking at the rows and rows of brides in white dresses and men in uncomfortable suits. The noise rivalled a chicken coop. Some days the department is dealing with as many as a hundred and seventy couples. By the entrance, vagrants offer their services as witnesses. In the centre of the space, photos can be taken in front of a three foot tall picture of the White House. Wedding photographers can be hired for two dollars per photo. No rings? No problem. A stand offering jewellery, and even veils, is the answer. The man with the pre-packaged bouquets is also doing a great trade.

We surveyed this wedding factory and loved it. Two more weeks and we would be kicking off the greatest adventure of our lives.

=

I wear her jumper, shirt, t-shirts, and her All Stars that have become a little lopsided with use. I don't care what I look like. It once seemed like a good idea to get rid of all our things. Now I desperately hold on to the few things I have

left. I wear her socks, her underwear. I can't wear her jeans.
Our bodies are too different.

She bought her clothes in the men's department. Because
she thought she looked better in them, but also because her
physique wasn't suited to women's clothes. No hips, little
waist. A gorgeous boy body, I thought. Too-big breasts and
too-narrow shoulders, she thought.

How can you be so beautiful and not even know it, I often
asked her?

She had a love-hate relationship with clothes. Hated the
poor quality and impermanence. 'Later, when I grow up, I
want a closet full of only Tom Ford suits and shirts.' George
Falconer's closet in *A Single Man* was her wardrobe dream.
Huge quantities of identical suits and shirts. So that she'd
have something different to wear each day, without ever
having to wonder what. Clothes she could go out to dinner
in, but also wear to sit on the beach. A uniform for all occasions. All those clothes neatly ironed and nice-smelling in
the wardrobe. And that house from the film wouldn't be a
bad idea either. She later found the house on the Architecture
For Sale website and shelved the dream. It was in the woods,
and she didn't like that idea very much. You never knew who
or what was hiding behind a tree.

I wear her things in an attempt to take her with me. Every
day I wonder how that should be done, because until now
I'm just a person in oversized clothes. Even in men's clothes
I look feminine. In contrast to her, which always led to a
commotion at public toilets. In the friendliest situations, the
attendant would say she was mistaken. That the men's toilets

were on the other side. In most other situations there was screaming. Yes, screaming. As if screaming is required when a 'man' walks into a women's toilet. Julian regularly held in her pee for far too long because she didn't want to cause any 'hassle.' Once I figured that out, I usually went with her. Not because she couldn't take care of herself, but because I had a bigger mouth. What disturbed me the most was that Julian felt ashamed of it. Previous girlfriends had found this public toilet issue annoying. I asked her not to take it personally. But, it did make me mad that these kinds of incidents were part of her everyday reality.

TED speaker and activist Ivan Coyote recounts that they usually went to the men's toilet to prevent this kind of situation. Until, at some point, they were beaten up there. Since then, they've gone back to the women's toilets and tried to explain the situation. Annoying, but preferable to a beating. They are lobbying for the purchase of gender-neutral toilets.

After Julian's breasts were removed, her 'feminine assets,' as she jokingly called them, were completely gone. The screaming got louder, and I accompanied her to the toilet even more frequently. Those Tom Ford suits would now look better on her. That was an advantage. My wife was an optimist.

=

In 1928 the lesbian novel *The Well of Loneliness* by British writer Radclyffe Hall was published. The book tells the story of Stephen Gordon, an Englishwoman from a distinguished family whose 'inversion' was obvious from an early age.

The term 'inversion' was used by sexologists in the late nineteenth and early twentieth century to refer to homosexuality. According to them, this was due to an innate reversal of sex characteristics. For example, sexologist Richard von Krafft-Ebing described female sexual inversion as 'the masculine soul, heaving in the female bosom.' It was classified under the mental conditions as a 'degenerative disorder.'

In 1926, Radclyffe Hall was at the peak of her career and her book Adam's Breed was an award-winning bestseller. She knew *The Well of Loneliness* could put her fame on the line, but she was determined to break the public silence around homosexuality. She sought, and found, support from her partner, sculptor and translator Una Troubridge, and told her publisher not to change a single word of the book. Although *The Well of Loneliness* contained only one sexual reference – 'and that night, they were not divided' – a British court condemned it for defending 'unnatural practices between women.'

Hall was tried for obscenity. Leonard Woolf drafted a letter in protest. Virginia Woolf, George Bernard Shaw, and T.S. Eliot, among others, testified in Hall's defence and signed a petition against the censoring of writers. The judge nevertheless decided that the book should be destroyed.

In 1949 the book was re-released. *The Well of Loneliness* remains one of the most important lesbian novels in literary history. Radclyffe Hall and Una Troubridge stayed together. To complement Hall's masculine look, Troubridge had always preferred to dress in a feminine way. After Hall's death from colon cancer in 1943, she had her wife's suits altered so she could wear them herself.

=

'Red-haired girls ...' someone is singing behind me on the street. I turn to see an old man walking awkwardly with a stick.

'Barely able to walk, but what a flirt!' I take his arm.

I would never have done this earlier. I would have coyly laughed and kept walking. Now I ask him where he lives and if I could keep him company for a bit.

We talk about songs of the past and the present, and he wants to know if I was bullied at school for my red hair. He was happy to learn that I was not. Julian would have loved this. She often engaged in conversation with older people on the bus, or on a park bench. 'There's such a wealth of knowledge there,' she often said.

One of the initiatives she admired tremendously was the documentary project *Conversations with Gay Elders*. We had spoken with director David Weissman for *Et Alors?* about his documentary *The Cockettes*. About the rise (and fall) of hippies and drag queens in 1970s San Francisco. In his latest work, he talked to gay men ranging from seventy-two to eighty-six years of age, and had them tell their life stories. He had each video edited by a gay man between the ages of twenty and thirty. In doing so, he not only documented our pre-history, but he also launched an intergenerational dialogue.

What was it like, in the old days, for a gay man or woman? I, myself, have an uncle who was admitted to a psychiatric institution in the 1950s because of this 'disease.' These are stories of great importance. Not just to help us realise where we've come from, but also to recognise what we don't want to return to. As an individual, and certainly as a child, you need role models, and in homosexuality these are rarely found in the family line. Some people have ancestors who once stood on the barricades against slavery, or for women's suffrage. As a gay person you don't have those ancestors, because it is not a genetically transmitted trait. But, those people who paved the way, so that we can now walk hand and hand in some countries, really do exist. However, they are hardly part of a typical history lesson. Heroes such as Marsha P. Johnson, trans artist, activist, and one of the leading figures during the 1969 Stonewall uprisings. Barbara Gittings, founder of the first lesbian group, Daughters of Bilitis, in 1958. In the seventies Gittings was the one who convinced the American Psychiatric Association to stop labelling homosexuality as a mental disorder. Or the German judge Karl Heinrich Ulrichs, who in 1854 was forced to resign after openly stating – as one of the first people to do so – that he was gay. In 1867 he addressed the Congress of German Jurists in Munich to demand equal rights for homosexuality. And Simon Nkoli, anti-apartheid, gay rights, and HIV/AIDS activist, and organiser of the first Pride March in Johannesburg. He was instrumental in convincing the African National Congress to recognise gay rights in the country. 'If I have seen further, it is by standing on the shoulders of giants,' wrote Newton.

Meanwhile, I have walked the old man home, and he has told me about his loneliness since his wife died. I bite the inside of my cheek. I help him with the key and thank him for the conversation. 'Bye, strange girl,' he says, with a brief wave.

*On the surface it looks like we're just
dudes who are dressing up in too much
make-up and sparkly clothes, however
the stories we share on the show
resonate with many people.*

In conversation with Alaska,
Ru Paul's Drag Race
Et Alors? Magazine

THOSE WERE EXCITING TIMES, THAT LAST WEEK BEFORE THE
first wedding performance. Still so much work to do, including moving, time and again. Due to our financial constraints,
we had to make do with rentals found through various con-
tacts, and we moved nine times in those three months. This
time, we'd found something on Craigslist and we were sitting
in a fifteen-square-foot room above a Brooklyn pizza parlour.
My hair smelled like oregano. 'I want to devour you,' she said.

While for Julian, one person might be a satisfactory audience,
I was a little more practical by nature and reasoned that the
more press we got, the easier it would be to complete this
performance piece. I was a longtime fan of Noah Michelson.
He was an interesting activist and writer, and editorial director
at *The Huffington Post*. If he picked it up, we'd be well on our
way, I felt. Half an hour after my email, he sent a message back
saying that he would like to interview us.

The article went online a week before our first wedding.
During that time, the phone was tolerated at the dinner table,

as an exception, so I jumped up and hugged Julian amid the curry dishes. The owner of the Indian restaurant joined in with our exuberance and read the article aloud from behind the register. 'Compelling performance piece' and 'stunning' were words used in the feature. Is this really about us, we wondered in disbelief, our hearts uneasy with tension. The packed restaurant applauded and people came and hugged us. Julian and I were beaming. A little embarrassed, but over the moon.

I was proven right: after the article got published in *The Huffington Post*, we took off. The international press got hold of the story and even newspapers and magazines from countries where we were not allowed to marry wanted to interview us. *Jeanne Magazine* devoted four pages to 22 and hoped that Switzerland would be added to the list. Jeff Koons, Marina Abramović, and Siri Hustvedt sent their congratulations. We received reports from media outlets around the world asking when we were visiting their country. They would schedule the airtime accordingly.

How crazy is this, we said to each other.

Every morning we had to get up at five in order to get everything done. Heaps of emails, every morning. Messages requesting interviews, collaborations, photo shoots. We talked to journalists about the future, about the present, and about our dreams. We tried to pour everything into the present day and not to miss a second of the rollercoaster we were on. So much haste.

One morning I was in the bathtub when Julian came and perched on the edge of the toilet with a big smile. She'd gone and got us pizza for breakfast (just because she could), and a request had come in from *A Plus*, Ashton Kutcher's positive news site. I could feel her hands shaking as she rinsed the shampoo from my hair. Kutcher had congratulated us on social media before. 'Is it stupid that I think this is really cool?' she asked.

The phone never stopped ringing, until Julian was admitted to the hospital in France, three months later.

=

When I revisit the *A Plus* video I see so much joy. Such an appetite for life. We laugh a lot, unconsciously touching each other all the time, and talk about things we love to do and what we believe in.

By then my wife had fought so hard not to die. She loved living so much. The doctors were amazed that she had lived so actively for another eighteen months after her breast surgery, and said that in theory she could never have recovered, let alone do these kinds of projects. She did everything by sheer willpower. Until it literally ran out.

I, too, am very strict with myself and I quickly pass judgement that I must not whine, but act instead. Now, something has happened to me that is beyond my control. Which I have not chosen and can do nothing about.

One day I wake up and my first thought is that I *do* have a choice. I lie completely still and let the realisation flow through me. I have fallen, fallen hard, but I can get up or I can continue lying down. I will never be able to bring her back, no matter what I do. I will never stop being madly in love with my wife, but I can choose whether or not to get out of bed. What I do after that doesn't matter. Lie down. Get up. Limited options, but definitely a choice. I instinctively know that my whole future depends on this, so every day I choose to open my eyes and try to put my feet on the floor. Sometimes it works, sometimes it doesn't. But, I do it when I feel it's going to be a viable day, and also when I'd prefer to never wake up again. I do it when I am looking forward to something, and when I feel I will never have anything to look forward to. Getting up does not guarantee the end of my grief, quite the contrary. But it is an action. When life sometimes feels a little less dark, I try to hold on to the moment with all my might. Because I know that, in the next minute, it could be over.

I feel like I have been on the periphery
of society for most of my life.

In conversation with Martin(E) Gutierrez
Et Alors? Magazine

A WONDERFUL MAN WALKED UP TO US IN UNION SQUARE. AS if we had an appointment that had been arranged for centuries. He was wearing a tatty suit and reminded me of the *Thin White Duke*. He sat down next to us on the grass. Among the printouts of the 22 budget and the endless lists of all the people we still had to contact or call. The man said his name was Daniel. Before we could introduce ourselves, he said he knew who we were. He had read about us in the newspaper. I laughed and waited to see what would transpire. He put Julian's water bottle and our notebooks in my bag, handed me my sunglasses, and asked, 'Ready?' Julian and I followed him to the subway. Neither of us were surprised about what happened; this was New York. The ride was long and little was said. I looked out the window and had no idea where we were going.

There was a fierce sea breeze, and Coney Island was deserted. Most of the rides were still closed and the wooden roller coaster creaked eerily. Daniel led us between the carnival booths to the freak show theatre where he gave three shows a day.

'Look what I found,' he said to his friends, as if we were a couple of marbles. They nodded, as if they already knew about it. We sat on wooden bleachers that I felt we might fall through at any moment, and watched the dancing people with dwarfism and the fire-eaters. I pushed my face into Julian's neck when someone started doing something with weights that I didn't want to see. She put her hands over my ears to shut out the clamour, as well. The audience's screams sounded like the noise inside a seashell.

After wrestling his way out of a straitjacket three different ways, Daniel came back to sit with us. Did we want to spend the evening with them? They all lived in the storage rooms above the 'theatre.' They had soup. And bread.

The following morning, I woke up early to the sun shining brightly on my face. I was wearing a long, black wig and my face was touching Julian's. Daniel's hand lay on hers. That night I had learned their dances and counted someone's tattoos. We'd eaten soup, talked, and sung 'Karma Police' with the twins who tied themselves together during their shows, like they were Siamese. I quietly woke my wife and together we stepped over the sleeping bodies, and back into reality.

=

You only know what grieving is when you are in the middle of it. People talk about the loss of a parent, a sister, and claim to know how I feel. I listen to what they say, but I can't muster the energy to be interested. *You haven't lost Julian*, is all I can think. They don't wake up five times a night in a panic because their parent or sister is no longer lying next to them. I'm ashamed of my selfishness, and often berate myself. That I'm not the only one experiencing this. That stern voice is outside of me, preaching to the teary-eyed toddler inside. I am the only one who has experienced the worst. Everyone's life goes on and new tragedies and dramas arrive. Except for me. I'm still in the same place. Motionless while everything around me is once again going into overdrive. I can't commiserate with other people's problems. I'm too busy surviving.

People are bad at mourning, I notice. 'The Apache ignore widows. Fearing outbursts of grief, they pretend that those suffering from it don't exist,' Siri Hustvedt writes. I read stories about widows who are asked, after just two months, if they are 'over it.' Three months later they are accused of wallowing in their grief. I call myself 'widow' in order to defuse it. This is how I anticipate the impact this word has on me, forestalling the stabs it causes when it comes from someone else.

'You'll get over it.'

'You're still young, you'll find someone else.'

I wonder if people realise what they are saying.

'Are you doing a bit better today?'

But what do I want to hear? I don't know myself. I don't want pity, but neither do I wish to pretend to be stronger than I am. Most of all, I want her death to be taken seriously. I want to talk about her because I'm terrified that she will be forgotten. If something funny causes me to smile, I cover my mouth. I don't want people to think I'm over her already. That wouldn't do her justice. Sometimes, we are more considerate towards the dead than to ourselves.

It's appropriate to feel gratitude whenever people reach out. But, it remains difficult when everyone keeps telling me how strong I am. And that, if anyone can survive this, it will be me. What they don't know is that for every minute I hold it together in public, I have to work twice as hard when I get back home. Meekly passing through the checkout, I pay for an evening with friends with two days of seclusion. I have learned not to shed tears in people's presence. That's my only rule. Because it's the only time I can maintain the illusion of ever living a normal life again. So, I say, 'The food was delicious,'instead of screaming that I miss her. And, when I feel myself starting to slide off chairs again, I know I have to go home. There it is allowed. Because if I cried in public, I would never stop.

Being gay I think we're put in a position
where we have no choice than to be an
activist, and we learn to love that.

In conversation with Adore Delano,
Ru Paul's Drag Race
Et Alors? Magazine

A LOVE STORY LIKE THIS MUST BE MADE UP, I MUSED ON THE morning of our New York wedding. I woke up in a gigantic bed in the beautiful Wythe Hotel, a wedding present from the management. Turning my head to the right, I saw my sleeping wife. Turning to the left, I saw the entire Manhattan skyline.

And then it was seven o'clock, and the circus started. 'We're getting married today,' I whispered in her ear. She woke up with a big smile.

After six calls the girl at the front desk apologised for the transfer, but it never stopped. I gave live radio interviews and recorded answers that were later broadcast on television. New York, L.A., France, Belgium, the Netherlands, even Italy and Japan, where same-sex marriage was still illegal. They were all reporting. Meanwhile, Julian took a tranquil shower, got dressed, and commented on what I said. She left the talking to me because 'you do that much better.'

'Convenient for you!' I said.

In between interviews, I was trying to get dressed, inter-mittently jumping on and off the bed to expend excess energy, and lost my lipstick. When it came time to leave, she was looking pretty as a picture while I appeared to have crawled through a snowstorm.

Julian had been gifted a dark-blue custom suit by Suit Supply, I stuck to vintage. Some Tom Ford, some Chanel, and Zara shoes.

We purposely had not sent out a press release announcing the ceremony. This was the first time, and it was more important to be able to do our own recording for the documentary, stress-free. We had made an exception for a journalist from Vice who would make a video report. Apart from that, we were accompanied by Bubi Canal, an artist friend we had interviewed for *Et Alors?* a few years earlier, and who would take the wedding pictures. Bart and Peter, a great couple we had met in recent days, were our witnesses.

Michael McSweeney stood waiting for us near the line of couples anticipating their turn, and led us to an office where both we and the witnesses had to sign the certificates. Then, we were taken to a room with pale-green walls and nothing but a large, brown lectern in the centre. Julian installed our camera on the tripod and pinned microphones onto McSweeney and ourselves.

Both of us were nervously fiddling with our hands as a roaring voice announced the start of the three minutes. The ceremony went by in a daze and I felt as if I was in a movie when we uttered the words 'to be your lawfully wedded wife' and 'till death do us part.' With a 'by the power vested in me ...' we were married for real, and Julian had tears in her eyes. I held my hand to her face. The City Clerk took both of us in his arms and said he was proud to have had the opportunity to do this.

After the ceremony we walked all over New York with Bubi, for the photo shoot. By 10 p.m., we were lying, dog tired, next to each other in bed, watching the changing lights of the Chrysler Tower.

'We've made a start,' she said, and fell asleep. I packed our bags for Amsterdam and listened to her breathing until I saw the sun rise.

=

While doing 22, we had received so much press that people recognised us on the street.

'Are you ...?'

'Yes!' she would answer.

People said 'How wonderful' and 'Congratulations,' and 'Great job!' Two huge men dressed in leather, and with long beards said, 'Thank you.' The taller one lifted me off the ground and kissed my forehead.

Now, six months later, somebody recognises me on the street.

'Are you ... I read that she ...'

I nod and walk on.

It's raining, it's cold. If the world was still as it should be, we would now be in South Africa. The only country in Africa where we were allowed to get married. After our wedding in New York, we were contacted by a Dutch wedding consultant who wanted to help us with the African marriage. Iris showed us all the options we could choose from, suggested we marry surrounded by wildebeest (it would make for great pictures) and had even contacted a lesbian official who was eager to perform the ceremony. A friend of Iris' had come along and she wanted to show us the country. Cape Town, Johannesburg, Table Mountain, and a place called Welgevonden ('well found'), a name that made us very happy. I was hoping to borrow a dress from the South African fashion designer Palesa Mokubung.

I'm looking at the grey sky over Antwerp.

It's my dream to inspire in the same
way I've been inspired by the work of
others. Ideally, my creations could be a
catalyst for positivity.

In conversation with Bubi Canal
Et Alors? Magazine

OUR SECOND MARRIAGE TOOK PLACE IN AMSTERDAM. ALL THE ceremonies seamlessly fell into place, and we went from one rush to the next, across a few different time zones. In New York, a mere hour before our departure, we gave another interview for *Chasing News*, and had to walk in and out of a park with a reporter, just to get the picture right.

At Schiphol airport the press was already waiting for us. It made me laugh uncontrollably, and Julian put my big sunglasses on my nose and told me to 'do a Victoria Beckham'. News of our performance had spread quickly, and in Amsterdam we were surrounded by a large number of people who aimed to make our trip as pleasant as possible. Our friends Robert and René had offered us their beautiful apartment for two weeks, and we drove straight from the airport to the ateliers of LeonLeon. A year earlier, Dutch designer Leon Klaassen Bos had celebrated his company's 'coming out' by publicly speaking out in favour of same-sex marriage. Friends had been pointing out to him that the average bridal shop didn't know what to do with two men or two women. Consequently, most boutiques would recommend identical outfits. A gap in the market. Leon had contacted us in New York, and asked if he could design our clothes for the Amsterdam wedding.

Photographer Femke van Hettema had also sent an email, offering to take photos of the ceremony. When we met, she told us how her childhood in Friesland had traumatised her. Raised in a strict family, within an evangelical church community, she'd first attempted to come out when she was thirteen. What followed were pastoral conversations and prayers, with the aim of 'liberating' Femke from her lesbian orientation. Psychological torture packaged as Christian care. They prayed for her: for deliverance from the 'unclean thoughts' that were not divinely-inspired; for deliverance from the devil, who would lure her away from God. It was an indoctrination that made her feel both dirty and unworthy. Harmful to a young teenager who was just starting to discover and learn about life, her body, love, and sexuality. Something that, years later, led to severe anxiety, trauma, and depression.

Ten years after she first tried coming out, Femke made a second attempt, because by now she had a girlfriend. No exorcism this time, but excommunication instead. Her social circle, which had always consisted of people from the Church, completely disappeared.

Meanwhile, Femke has found a new circle of friends and has completely let go of her faith. However, she continues to carry the trauma, something she talks about publicly, because 'after all, we all know what it feels like to be marginalised.'

We listened in horror to her story, and admired the woman she had become. Once again, we were surrounded by people who strengthened our belief that there was still much work to be done.

Amsterdam was an important marriage for Julian. When she was little, she had been told she would never be able to marry a girl. Now, it was possible. Since April 1, 2001. And, proudly she strode, in her black tuxedo, up to the altar, where I was waiting for her in a long white dress. It turned into an emotional day, made even more so by being reunited with our friends, and the throng of press folks who flocked around us, but reported extensively and positively on our performance. After the ceremony, the City of Amsterdam treated us to coffee and cake. That day we were followed by three different news channels, and during the two weeks we were in Amsterdam, we were invited to the studios of *Koffietijd* and RTL Late Night, where Humberto Tan poured champagne for us and had a purple cake delivered during the show.

*I feel it's important to consider whatever
particular identity an artist embraces
– whether that relates to their gender,
sexual orientation, ethnicity, etc. – in the
hope it will challenge and expand a
viewer's perspective on their art.*

Michael Schreiber on Bernard Perlin
Et Alors? Magazine

THE ANTWERP WEDDING, ON THE OTHER HAND, WAS MY HOME game. Once again, we went from one interview to the next and got together with friends, all the while trying to arrange the ceremonies, transportation, clothing, and accommodation for the countries which were to follow. I noticed that Julian was getting worn out. More often, I was the one who was already answering emails at six a.m. while she lingered in bed a bit longer. She often had headaches, which she never used to have, and felt tired. So tired, sometimes, that it made her dizzy. I wondered if we had started the performance too soon. If she had sufficiently recovered from her surgery.

Friends recommended an Ayurvedic practitioner. He examined her, asked questions, and decided she wasn't properly absorbing the necessary vitamins from her food; that something was wrong with her digestion. He gave her three kinds of preparations. For the morning, the afternoon, and the evening. 'These are strong pills, so you could suffer some unpleasant side effects for a while.' Chances were that the symptoms would get worse before they got better, that's how it worked with Ayurvedic remedies. So, we were not fazed when she had even less energy and her headaches didn't disappear. 'That's how it works,' we said. 'It gets worse at first.'

I have trouble remembering how we spent our days in Antwerp. I can picture our enthusiastic friends during the ceremony, and the beautiful dress I had borrowed from the designer Tim Van Steenbergen. But, a fog obscures the many conversations we had, during the reception that the city had organised for us. Except that everyone said that Julian looked so tired. And asked if she was doing alright. We did a photo session for the magazine Feeling, in which we danced beneath a shower of golden confetti, and to which they later added the headline '2018, Year of Celebration!'. These memories were diminished by the rising sense of anxiety that something was about to happen, and which both of us were trying to suppress. Without consulting her, I had started looking for an opportunity to postpone our fifth wedding, in Spain, for a few weeks. Both Barcelona and Madrid wanted to welcome us, and I decided to calmly wait until a consensus was reached. We didn't care which city the ceremony would take place in, as long as it was in Spain.

I asked her if I should cancel Paris, but she wouldn't hear of it. Paris would take place, the ceremony had been arranged to perfection with the help of the Dutch Consulate, and she did not want to change that. After Paris, we would go to my mother's place for her seventieth birthday. We decided to stay with her a little longer. Julian could convalesce while I organised the next series of weddings. Before we knew it, she'd be on top form again.

=

Peter Orlovsky was twenty-one, and working as a painter's model for Robert Lavigne, when Allen Ginsberg walked into his studio in 1954. The story goes that the godfather of the Beat Generation fell in love with the subject of *Nude With Onions (Portrait of Peter Orlovsky)*, even before actually meeting the model. Shortly after they met, they moved in together and talked openly about their relationship, which they regarded as a marriage, half a century before this topic even entered the political agenda. Given their fame, they became the first 'married' gay couple many people had heard of. On their alternative ceremony, Ginsberg wrote, 'The moment we looked into each other's eyes, a kind of heavenly fire descended on us. It ignited, illuminated the entire cafeteria and transformed it into an eternal space.'

Two years after their first encounter, Ginsberg, inspired by Orlovsky, published *Howl and Other Poems*, in which he wrote openly about eroticism and homosexuality. His publisher was charged with obscenity, but later acquitted.

Their relationship was turbulent; steeped in drugs and alcohol, they lived the beat lifestyle in Paris, but also travelled the world. In the 1960s and 1970s they organised, and participated in, demonstrations for gay rights and the legalisation of marijuana. Madness followed them wherever they went, and they wrote, lectured, experimented with language and drugs in the company of junkies, fellow writers, misfits, and bohemians. They stayed together for forty-three years. Orlovsky's health deteriorated after Ginsberg's death in 1997. Having lost his anchor and compass, the lifelong battle with his demons returned in all its fury, making him unstable. Nevertheless, he continued to organise beat events and demonstrations until his death in 2010.

He was buried next to Ginsberg in Colorado.

I think it's part of our culture that
everyone wants to know exactly what
they are looking at and why.

In conversation with Martin(E) Gutierrez
Et Alors? Magazine

JULIAN SLEPT THROUGHOUT THE ENTIRE TRAIN JOURNEY
from Antwerp to Paris. I had trouble waking her upon arrival.
In our friend Renaud's apartment at Les Halles, she sat on
the terrace in the winter sun. She still had a headache, and
was exhausted. In retrospect, it's incredible how we kept on
dismissing her fatigue, but after all, we'd been working for a
few months now, without taking a break, so it made sense.
She said she felt a little overworked, and was looking forward
to resting up at my mother's place.

'Sorry to be such a whiner,' she said.

'You're not a whiner. You're just tired,' I replied. And, I
kissed her on the head.

She was reading Malcolm Gladwell's *The Tipping Point*.
I was cooking. Roasted sweet potatoes with courgette and
porcini mushrooms. Looking back, I'm amazed that I can
still remember these kinds of details.

I set the table and went to check on her. Normally, she
would have walked into the kitchen more than once by now,
to read to me. The book she was reading was about the

critical moment when 'the ball gets rolling.' A topic that fascinated her, and about which she had a lot to say. That day she remained silent.

She sat on the patio, staring straight ahead.

'The letters are moving,' she said.

Suddenly tears were running down my face. I wiped them away, anxious and ashamed. She kissed my hand.

'Don't worry.'

The next two days we stayed indoors a lot. She thought the streets were too busy, and I started organising our South American itinerary, which would begin after the Spanish ceremony. We went out just once, to meet our photographer Mahdi. Mahdi Aridj is from Algeria and had lived in Paris for several years. A beautiful man, with wonderful stories about his origins. He was the kind of man Julian clicked with. My wife liked tough, empathetic, intelligent men. And, that kind of man loved her, too. Men with whom she formed a camaraderie from the first moment, who'd slap her on the back, but gently. 'Great buddies' was an expression that often came to mind when I saw it happen. We were baffled when Mahdi told us that Algeria has an agreement with the French authorities which stipulates that gay Algerians are not allowed to marry in France. I thought of George Orwell: 'All animals are equal, but some animals are more equal than others.' Even in a country where same-sex marriage is accepted, there are still loopholes to get around the law.

The day of the wedding I didn't have my eye on the ball. The green silk dress with the dozens of buttons, another design by LeonLeon, was ready, and her suit was pressed. Julian was standing, somewhat hunched over, in the bathroom. Normally, my wife always stood up straight. I asked her if I should cancel. 'No, no,' she said. It would be okay; she was just so very tired.

We took a taxi to the town hall. Mahdi was ready for us, as were the Dutch consulate people and a few press folks. I was absentmindedly making small talk, trying to keep a constant eye on Julian. She came to be by my side, and leaned heavily against me. On the tall staircase to the ceremonial hall, I took her hand. She asked if I could walk a bit slower.

We were married by Hélène Bidard, the mayor's deputy, who was responsible for gender equality and human rights. A perfect combination.

France was the ninth country in Europe, and at that time the fourteenth country in the world, to approve same-sex marriage. When President Hollande signed the law on May 18, 2013, more than 150,000 people angrily took to the streets of Paris. The city of romance was overrun with hate that day. Fundamentalists of every kind, who in any other situation would be bashing each other's brains in, now shared half a banner each for the 'greater cause'. If it weren't so shocking, it would border on slapstick.

Julian positioned our camera, and for the first time I checked whether it was properly adjusted. She didn't seem to notice. Everything was correct.

I was happy to be there with her, for the fourth time. I was grateful all those people had gone to such great lengths to help us, but I didn't hear anything that was said. I could see she was having trouble keeping herself upright. She was pale. I had to keep swallowing, so as not to be sick.

After saying, 'I do,' I felt relieved. Now we could go home, I could put her to bed, brew some tea, and take care of her until she got better. But she wanted to have pictures taken first. 'We need those,' she said.

We took a taxi with Mahdi to Place des Vosges. The sun was shining, the park was beautiful, but I only had eyes for my wife, who needed my help to walk, as if she were drunk.

=

Five months after her death, I received an offer to speak about our work in Paris. I felt the city needed exorcising. This is where I saw my wife falter. It was here I saw for the first time how she'd get a strange look in her eyes, every now and then. As if she didn't know where she was from one moment to the next. Then, she'd put her arms around me for support and reassurance.

We had given many lectures in recent years. About our work, and about positive activism. I enjoyed doing it and, although I was the one talking and not Julian, I wondered if I'd be able to do it without her being near, and getting her feedback afterwards. I'm not ready to go to Paris, but I know I have to do this in order to take a step forward. It is essential to overcome these kinds of hurdles. If I let them grow, the chances are I'll never clear them again. I am determined to keep pushing myself towards the future. And, I need to make a living; that too.

Paris is even more emotionally devastating than I imagined, and the first day there I walk through the city sobbing behind a pair of big sunglasses. I can manage having a drink, but not eating out, by myself. So, I live on fruit and chocolate. I watch the passers-by from a café terrace. Couples, not all of them happy. Why them and not us? A non-question, but one I ask myself nonetheless. For a long time, I watch a man draw a picture of a dog. It's a hideous drawing, with a lot of yellow, orange and brown. The dog is squinting. A couple, who are walking by, stop. They speak to the artist and watch the dog become even uglier. To my amazement, they buy the piece. The drawing is rolled up and put into a blue tube, and the husband walks towards the toilet of the bar where I am sitting. As soon as he's out of sight, the woman and the artist are drawn to each other as if by a magnet. They kiss. Passionately. I look around me in amazement. Am I the only one seeing this? The other people on the terrace are too busy talking to each other. When the man returns, they act as if nothing has happened and say goodbye, thanking the artist effusively for the beautiful artwork, and carry on walking. Fact is stranger than fiction, and if I read this scene in a book, I would never believe it.

I meet up with Mahdi. It's still difficult to look at his photos of our wedding. In hindsight, I can see how ill she is, and how my gaze is one of unadulterated panic. I ask him if he could sense anything that day. He says that he knew something bad was about to happen. Julian died on his birthday; he was the last person to take photos of us together. He's projecting a great deal of emotion onto the event.

We sit on iron chairs in the Tuileries Garden and watch the people at the funfair. People screaming out in free fall. Revived by mortal fear. Mahdi talks about his childhood in Algeria. The loss of friends and family. About how, one day, just like any other day, he went to bring food to his grandmother. Only, that time he was running a few minutes late, and due to this he just managed to avoid a bomb blast on the road.

'Nothing is certain,' he says. 'Every day that I wake up is a bonus.'

Julian said the same thing after her surgery. I hear it and know what he means, but I don't feel it. Not anymore. He tells me to surrender to it. 'You can't possibly know what's going to happen, so why try?' He calls me a control freak.

I tell him the story of the ugly dog. 'And then?' I ask. I'm taken aback by the hysteria in my voice. 'Then you get home with that awful portrait – it's not even your own dog. Then what?'

He looks at me. 'But every time they see that drawing, they remember that nice day in Paris. And the woman will often remember the artist. How cool is that?'

We look at two children holding giant pink and blue candyfloss. He takes my hand. 'You know, it's okay not to know how to live for a while. That way you can't make any mistakes.'

*As an artist you have to live with the fact
that people project their own horrors,
joys and everyday life issues onto your
work. That's the beauty about being a
performer.*

In conversation with The Vivid Angel
Et Alors? Magazine

I CANCELLED OUR PARIS INTERVIEWS AND WE GOT THE TRAIN
to my mother's place in the South of France. A week earlier
than planned, as Julian was too tired to do anything else. My
mother had organised a big party for her seventieth birthday,
and Julian wanted to get her health back by then. She assumed everything would be fine if she could just sleep for a
week. From our Paris apartment to the station, four train
changes, and then further on by bus and car to the house. In
my memory, the trip was a juggling act, with two large
suitcases, some hand luggage, and my wife leaning against
me. I helped her on and off the train each time, put her in a
seat, and went back and forth a few times to get all our stuff
on board. On the train I tried to arrange everything so that
our suitcases didn't get in anybody's way, while simultaneously keeping Julian upright, and trying to keep my face
looking as calm as possible.

After an eleven-hour journey, we finally arrived at the
house and I struggled to help her up the stairs to our bedroom. I undressed her and tucked her in under the sheets.

'Give me a week,' she said. 'I'll be better by your mama's birthday.'

'Don't stress,' I said.

Within a second, she fell asleep. I nervously roamed the house and phoned my mother who was on holiday, but had decided to come home straight away. The house had been sitting empty for a few weeks, and I felt the cold tiles under my bare feet, and shivered at the blackness outside the windows. The house stands alone, and the nearest neighbour is a fifteen-minute walk away. I looked up the number of the ambulance and the address of the nearest hospital, in case something happened. It turned out to be an hour's drive away. Hearing a sound coming from the bedroom, I ran up the stairs. Julian was sitting on the edge of the bed, looking at me with blank eyes. I asked what it was, but she didn't answer. I asked if she had to go to the bathroom. She nodded. I helped her up, and walked her to the bathroom. She was shaky and heavy, and I had to use all my strength to keep her from falling against the wall.

Things only got worse from that night on. Meanwhile, my mother had arrived and found scraps of paper all over the place, on which I'd scribbled notes: 'She can't go up the stairs on her own.' 'Nausea.' 'Can't get stronger because she can't keep food down!!!!' 'Ginger with salt against vomiting.' 'Chai tea (digestion!!!!) with almond milk. Recipe: ...'

Whole pages of easily digestible foods, tea for nausea, green juices to make her stronger. Lists were my way of getting a grip on the future. It didn't help.

I wanted to call a doctor, but she vehemently resisted. 'I just need to sleep it off for a bit,' she said. 'It's just a really bad flu. Just give me some time.' I gave in. But, I also said I would definitely call if it got any worse.

Three days after our arrival she turned forty, and I woke her up with a song. Gently, because it took her a while to become aware. I put her in the shower and helped her get dressed. Together, we descended the stairs with great difficulty. Her one arm heavy around me, the other hand on the bannister. Stair by stair. Excruciatingly slow. I carefully lowered her into a chair at the large wooden kitchen table, and heard my mother light a fire in the fireplace next door. I had bought her a bottle of Tom Ford perfume. She was never one to covet things, but perfume was the kind of luxury she loved. She looked at the package without doing anything.

'Go ahead and open it,' I said, as if to a child. She struggled with the ribbon and wrapping paper until I realised she was doing everything with her left hand. My wife was right-handed, but that hand was hanging limply by her side, without her noticing. I asked why she didn't use her other hand. She looked at it obliviously, then just carried on using her left hand.

I remember going to find my mother in the living room. 'We need to call a doctor,' I said. 'She's dying.'

Until today I have no idea where that knowledge came from, but I knew that life was grounding to a halt. There. In that moment.

=

Our personalities determine how we mourn. I have a tough, future-oriented core that leaves little room for downtime. I keep reading, searching, making connections, and then give myself permission to grieve. For my beloved, but also for the person I loved being but can never be again. The way I eat has changed (all day long, little snacks, standing, straight out of the fridge). The way I watch a film has changed (alone, restlessly, getting up all the time because I can't focus, rewinding because I can't focus). My circle of friends has changed (some I never hear from, others have turned into indispensable heroes). My job status has changed (the job disappeared with her). One's confidence changes (I can't do this without her). One's breathing changes (how do I do this again?). One's mindset changes, one's hobbies, interests, self-esteem, sense of humour, sense of security. One's brain also changes. And, unfortunately, I can tell you how that feels. Her death blocks my actions. Blocks my thinking. It's called 'Widow Brain.' It sounds dark, murky, full of gunk. Screeching voices in too-small rooms. Nails pressing into your skin until it bleeds, to feel a pain other than the one that's so excruciating. It turns out that's not it. Widow brain is a side effect of traumatic loss, where your mind is trying to protect you from the pain. Strangely enough, you forget everything except the pain it tries to protect you from. I stop talking mid-sentence, because I can't remember where I was going. I walk in and out of rooms, not knowing what I needed to do there. I am incapable of making the smallest decision. It leaves me with the feeling that I no longer have control over anything, in a world where I no longer have control over anything. Buddhist Pema Chodron writes, 'When we feel cornered, our minds tend to shrink.' Another name for it is 'grief-induced amnesia.'

It's hard to get away from the idea that my future should have been different. I want to appreciate life once more, but too much has been destroyed for me to hope with an open mind that I could ever attain my previous happiness again. I now know that statements like: 'You will learn something from it' are a myth. A false promise. All I learn from this is that I now see what life is really like. That it has no deeper meaning or purpose, but that it's you who decides whether to make something out of it or not. Whatever I choose has nothing to do with life, or the path I must follow, but with a decision that I make, and the meaning I myself give to it. I am only now realising how deluded I was to believe that there's a reason for everything, outside of ourselves. A beautiful illusion, it's true. But, nevertheless, just a fabric plaster. Life is. Period.

My friends, too, are grieving. And, now and then, this takes me by surprise. When Renate talks about Julian, she sometimes gets teary-eyed. It's good to know I am not the only one who misses her, that other people, too, wish she was still here. Julian's death has made many people think. About the finiteness of life, and about the importance of love. About their plans, their goals, and their future. Hence, one couple among our friends has finally embarked on a lengthy trip around the world. Other friends have called off the purchase of a house, because isn't it better to enjoy life a little more than to be paying off a mortgage for thirty years? Someone else finally decided to make their dream come true, by launching a clothing collection. Upon Julian's death, my mother and her husband took a closer look at their relationship and decided to call it quits, after eighteen years. She moved from France to Frigiliana, which she had lost her heart to since the first time she came to visit us. My mother is learning Spanish at seventy-two, and talks with the villagers about the thriving of the avocados. And that the oranges are in urgent need of rain.

I myself am starting the most challenging part of this book: the six weeks between Julian's diagnosis and her death. 'Writing is not life, but I think that sometimes it can be a way back to life,' wrote Stephen King.

My body refuses to cooperate. Once again, I feel an urge to go and lie on the floor. When I've written half a page, I can feel my hands getting heavy. My muscles go slack, and I can barely keep my eyes open. When I lie down, I sleep nonstop for twelve to fourteen hours. It's a familiar experience: I used to fall asleep whenever I was stressed. Insomnia would be more productive, I think to myself, the next time I emerge from my coma at 10 p.m. after I'd started writing at 8 a.m. but had to give up. My body's still doing its own thing and telling me when it's had enough. I listen and adjust my rhythm, writing my half pages at night. That way, I at least don't sleep my day away. Those times when I do manage to work for more than half an hour, I suddenly get itchy and become covered in a red rash that disappears half a day later. My rebellious body.

I want to be that kid who is lost in Oz,
looking for the wizard and believe that
it's all real.

In conversation with Christopher Logan
Et Alors? Magazine

THE VILLAGE DOCTOR CALLED AN AMBULANCE AND I HELPED
Julian get dressed. Her right hand hung limply at her side.
I took her hand, stretched my arm out alongside hers, and
up the sleeve of her sweater until it fit. She said her nails
were dirty. This was not the case. I brought her the nail
clippers and she laboriously clipped the nails on her right
hand. She forgot about the other hand. I would do that
later. When the doctor came to say that the ambulance was
on its way, he looked with resignation from the nail clippers
to me. I think I knew for sure at that point. That none of it
mattered anymore. I closed my eyes to what should have
been so obvious and hurried to pack our things. Both our
things. Because, I had no intention of leaving her alone for
a second. Passports, our Spanish insurance card, underwear, toothbrush.

'This is not right,' said the doctor, after examining her
eyes. 'There's something wrong with her brain.'

'It's come back,' she said.

'We can't be sure about that,' I said.

We waited downstairs for the ambulance, and I noticed she was becoming a bit more alert than she'd been that morning. Maybe nothing is wrong after all, I thought. She looked so awake.

'You called the doctor too soon,' she said. 'I feel much better already.'

She willingly allowed herself to be buckled down in the ambulance, as I was made to sit in the front. She stretched out her left hand and I held it between the seats.

At the hospital she was immediately placed under a scanner. Meanwhile, my mother had also arrived and we were given some chairs in a small waiting room. I was anxious and sad. I knew how worried she was feeling right then and I was not with her to relieve that fear. As they wheeled her into the waiting room, the doctor asked us to have patience until he got the results. It could take a while. I saw how upset she was and how hard she was trying to keep it together, so I suggested we meditate. At the foot of the mountain in Frigiliana there was an organic farm where we shopped twice a week. José, the founder of the cooperative, had approached Julian shortly after her breast surgery, and said he sensed she was very angry. And was he right? He listened to her story and asked if we'd ever heard of transcendental meditation (TM). All we knew about it was that David Lynch did it. And Russell Brand. That it was introduced to the west by maharishi Mahesh Yogi, in the 1950s, in India. That the Beatles had put it on the map. We knew what it was. We had toyed with the idea some time earlier, and then rejected it because of all the hype. Like the red Kabbalah strings that everyone wore after Madonna tied them around her wrist. However, José had made her curious. He had learned the technique firsthand from the maharishi, and told Julian it would change her life. Always motivated by a great story, we both agreed to learn it. After the shop's closing time we sat on the floor in a small room at the farm, for five evenings. In front of us was an altar with flowers. The fragrance of herbs, incense, and the metallic undertone of the air-conditioning. Outside it was 42°C. José taught us about the origins of TM and the scientific basis for its positive effects. Then he showed us how, by repeating a mantra in thought, we could make it go quieter until we were just conscious. Body and mind relax, and stress is reduced. During a ritual initiation, for which we had to bring flowers and incense, we were each assigned our individual mantra. A meaningless sound with the sole purpose of having a beneficial effect on the nervous system. Once we completed the classes, we were expected to do this for twenty minutes, twice a day. In the morning after our shower, and a second time in the afternoon. José had been right. Meditation effectively changed our lives. Everything calmed down, there was less stress, and after a while Julian even slept better. An energy lull in the afternoon was replaced with a renewed energy boost after the meditation. We were convinced.

'Let's meditate,' I said after she returned from the scanner. She nodded. A few seconds later she looked at me in alarm and said she had forgotten her mantra. I swallowed the bile and gave her mine.

=

'Grief turns out to be a place none of us know until we reach it,' wrote Joan Didion. Her husband, the writer John Dunne, died of a heart attack. They had worked together for 40 years. I recognise myself in these words. You think you know sorrow, that you know what it is. Until half of you is cut away and you find yourself staring blankly at an empty wall.

Sometimes I forget she's gone. Several times I've caught myself looking up from a book to tell her something she'd have found interesting. Then I have to close my mouth like a fish. I'm surprised how many times I want to ask her opinion on things. Which photo should I send for a programme booklet? Should I shorten my talk or not? Is this a good idea? How can I realise it? But also, all these films, exhibitions, music, and books that keep coming out, now that she is no longer there. Which I know she would have loved, but which we can no longer talk about. I miss her opinions, her judgement. For seven years we lived with each other's voices, supported by each other's benchmarks. Take one away, and everything falters.

Almost imperceptibly, the future creeps into my agenda and I find myself strenuously resisting it. She fell in love with me because I knew how to be free. Now I face a future in which I have to redefine that freedom. What do I still want, now that I have to carry on without Julian? From a distance I survey the reconstruction of a human being who resembles me outwardly, but who has grown centuries older within a few months. I have to investigate whether this new person has any chances of survival in a Julian-less world. In part, I am busy organising my life and making plans, until the next wave of grief washes everything away and I have to start all over again. I know I have a number of things on my schedule: the deadline for this book, a number of lectures, and the hosting of a literary salon at the Queer Arts Festival in Antwerp. But, until it happens, I cannot imagine what it will be like. It's as if my brain will only allow me to think in the short term, and these plans are just words in my planner. A curator would like the photo of our wedding in Antwerp to be part of an exhibition at Bozar in Brussels. I'm supposed to feel something now, I think, it's an important exhibition. But, I feel nothing. I just feel sick because I can't tell her. I'm shaken to realise how well I know what I don't want. While, everything I do want is scrupulously hidden behind a single sentence: *I want her back.*

=

On 14 March 2018, Brazilian politician and activist Marielle Franco was shot to death. Franco was committed to the fight against sexual violence, and for the rights of the LGBTQ+ community. Her party, PSOL, was the only party to openly oppose the aggressive actions of the military police. Franco was the first woman from the Brazilian slums to enter into politics. The fact that she was also black, and a lesbian, caused consternation.

Marielle Franco had been in a relationship with Monica Benicio for fourteen years, and they had planned to get married in 2019. Every month, Benicio takes to the streets with a large number of people to save her wife's ideology from being lost. Benicio, who is a social-housing architect, told journalist Joanie de Rijke: 'It has been ten months since Marielle was murdered, and I never thought I would follow in her footsteps. But, her death stirred up so much in the Brazilian people that I put in the spotlight willy-nilly, so I decided I had no choice but to continue Marielle's work and realise her dreams. It's an extreme way to live, but I consider it an honour. It also gives me the feeling that the bond between Marielle and I still matters, instead of just fading away. Marielle is the love of my life. We have had to keep our relationship a secret for more than ten years, under pressure from the prevailing homophobia in the country. Now that she's gone, I have found activism to be a reason to live.'

Meanwhile, more women have followed suit, but they all fear for their lives under the regime of President Bolsonaro, who has made sure there's no longer anyone representing the rights of LGBT people under his government. Brazil has the highest murder rate of LGBTQ+ people. Violence against vulnerable and minority groups is encouraged by the state.

=

One of the programs I once made while working in television was called *Levensgevaar* (Mortal Danger). We'd recreate deadly accidents, in which at least one person survived. I would interview the survivors. I scoured the newspapers for articles telling a local story with lots of drama and detail, and then paid a visit to the person in question. The budget for the program was dismal, so I had to personally convince the police to shut down a stretch of motorway in order to have a stunt team flip over a car a couple times. Or, the camera-man and I would fly over the sea in a helicopter, looking for a captain who'd let us land and then agree to star in a story about a sinking ship. I searched and found a Russian drilling platform where the men were elated by the distraction. I asked the entire crew to take a leaning stance near the railing (the ship in the story sank), and move slowly forwards, as if they were sailing through deep water. Despite the language barrier, I got the message across after a while, and ended up waving a garden hose behind the camera to mimic the rain. A grey filter, put on the images afterwards, created a bleak effect over the sunny day. I had makeup artists recreate the most gruesome burns, and hung high in the air on a military base with that same cameraman, to film a paragliding accident.

Organising and producing that program suited me, be-cause I enjoy bouncing from one adventure to the next. Not through fear of missing out, but out of wonder and curiosity. Even before the White Rabbit arrives, and I've heard him say, 'Oh my ears and whiskers, how late it's getting!' I'm al-ready on his trail.

Fear of experiencing something is completely foreign to me, yet has to be addressed constantly since Julian's death. 'I think fear must be the most interesting emotion we have. We are so often occupied with it,' Tennessee Williams wrote in his journals. He made the choice to drink away his fear. 'Fear, after all, is our real enemy,' added Christopher Isherwood. The fact that fear is all in our head gives me the motivation, not to give in to it, but to go along with it. What then follows is an exhausting battle. There is fear of flying, fear of travelling, fear of getting in a lift. Sometimes even fear of going out into the street to shop for groceries. And, one by one, I put them under the magnifying glass with which I examine my emotions.

There is also fear of writing, and sometimes I put it off for so long that I once went through the entire New York street map on Google Earth, read Take That's Wikipedia page, and eventually landed on a YouTube interview with Beyoncé's great-nephew. Those are productive days. Later on, I notice that, with writing it's not so much about fear, but rather about overcoming sadness. And, that I have to go back in time for a while to fully understand this myself. When I first met Jeroen, I had just written my first book (never published, not good either) and I was working on my second. For as long as I can remember, I've always wanted to be a writer (and a circus artist, but that's a different story). But, Jeroen was the writer and I was young, impressionable, and inse-cure, so I quit. For the sake of clarity, I'd like to add that he did nothing to make me do this. I sabotaged myself all by myself, and without the assistance of anyone else. Something that, years later, my feminist self is not very proud of. I still wrote a lot, but only press releases for artist and musician friends, which evolved into interviews. First in print, later for television. When Julian and I started *Et Alors?* I came into my own a bit more, and she encouraged me to start writing again. Confidently. Before she died, I promised her I would write this book. It carries a lot of baggage with it. On the one hand, there is the fear of the raw memories and the fatality of everything that happened. But, there is also sadness, because she will never be able to read this. Because I will write the only story. Which isn't necessarily a false story, but it is one-sided. I find that terribly sad.

Our uniqueness lies in the symbioses.
It's the chemistry between us, and in
our daily personal life, that shows in
our work.

In conversation with The Brothers Grimm
Et Alors? Magazine

THE DOCTOR WHO DID THE SCAN CAME IN WITH A WORRIED face, and asked if he could speak to me and my mother in the hallway. He said white spots were visible in her head which needed more detailed examination. He was sure it could be treated with radiotherapy. That follow-up scan could only be done a few days later. What she had to do very urgently, however, was take medication for epileptic seizures because, apparently, she'd been having those all the time. Unnoticed.

They would keep her in the hospital for further examination.

Julian nodded resignedly when I told her what the doctor had said, and also when I said they were going to make her better. That a solution would be sought. I followed the nurse, and the hospital bed with Julian in it, to the room and stated that I would be staying with her.

'Impossible,' they said.

'Just try and get me out of here,' I said.

I dislike scenes, drama, or making a fuss, but my wife no longer knew where she was at night, so I was prepared to scream the entire hospital down. After starting an IV, the nurse brought out a camp bed and a blanket. When I fell asleep that night, I dreamt of rabbits eating their young.

Waking up next to her was one of the best things about those seven years. There was no static interfering with my joy. My happiness was one of limitless possibilities, combined with a love that needed no questioning. She was. Present in every part of me. I felt her in my skin, in my bones.

When she became ill, it seemed that we were merging. At night I'd wake up when she had to go to the bathroom. Even before she woke up herself. Then, I would watch her, waiting. After a while she'd slowly open her eyes. I helped her out of bed. Sometimes, she would fall against me and I had to both hold her up and make sure the needles stayed put. Slowly and carefully, I walked her to the small bathroom while she looked at me, smiling and wide-eyed. I could see that she wasn't quite conscious, but she trusted me completely and followed wherever I told her to put her feet. Sitting, peeing, drying off, standing up, pulling up her briefs and turning around again in that tiny space, with one arm around her and the other around the IV stand. Tuck her in again, and make sure no stray limbs were hanging out of the bed. When she was cold, I would put my blanket over her and spend the night shivering. Every morning I forgot to ask the nurses for an extra blanket.

Her eyes are seared into my memory: big and sweet and completely oblivious to everything that was going on around her. Full of love, and completely trusting that I meant well for her. What a responsibility, I thought. For some reason, I found the thought that she wouldn't be prepared, if I wished her ill, unbearable.

Months later, that feeling returned when I was babysitting two cats in one of the places I rented. I walked from the kitchen to the living room carrying a bowl of soup, and one of the cats walked quietly beside me. I looked down at him and thought to myself that I could just drop that bowl on him, break his back, or badly burn it. Did he, like her, feel that I wanted the best for them?

=

And then, after a few months, there comes a moment when you suddenly get angry and want to burn the whole world down. It's so fierce it makes me tremble. I am angry with the physical humiliation she has endured. With life, for not realising what it would miss if she were no longer here. Next to me, on the tram a couple is arguing. They are furious. They say they'd like to smack each other, that he's a good-for-nothing, that she's so very stupid.

And they *are allowed to live*, goes through my mind. I have those days. More often than not. When I look at people and am angry that they are still there, with their quarrels, bored stares, and their resignation. Resigned to the lives they've stumbled into, and which they now have to make the best of.

'You're so angry,' says a friend, and suddenly I feel it. I didn't know. But, angry at what? And with whom? There is a part of me that feels love for every person I meet. But, there's also that violent streak, which makes me wish for everybody to experience what I'm going through. Just so I'll be understood.

Would it have been easier to deal with if she had died in a car accident? Then, at least I could have someone to blame. Give some direction to my emotion. Now I am angry with life, with reality. How do you avoid falling prey to a non-existent enemy?

I realise that I have to be more aware
of the amazing life that I am living.

In conversation with Sven Ratzke
Et Alors? Magazine

THE DAYS BEFORE THE ACTUAL DIAGNOSIS WERE BLURRY AND confused. I know there was a lot of apprehension, but I talked myself out of it. Or, I tried to. After the follow-up scan, we were told she had a large number of tumours in her brain. How many, the doctor couldn't yet say, but he told us they could still be treated with radiotherapy. He was also able to tell us that this had been going on for a long time, from even before her breast surgery, and he promised to request her medical records.

While she slept, I read about cancer and possible treatments. Most of the reports did not have a happy ending. I also tried to arrange a transfer to Spain. Our Spanish health insurance company was on the phone a few times a day, saying they wouldn't reimburse the costs in France. If she was transferred to Spain, then they would take care of everything. After an afternoon of searching, I found a hospital in Madrid where nutrition was also part of the treatment. I sent them an email asking if I'd be allowed to spend the night in her room. It was a Catholic hospital and, from experience with previous information requests, I already knew that this was not obvious for a gay couple. In the picture, the hospital looked like a luxurious retreat, with palm trees visible from the windows. Julian loved palm trees, and I somehow thought it important that I could give her that.

The doctor undid the hours of searching, by saying she could no longer be transported anywhere. That the pressure in her head would increase too much.

How am I going to pay for all of this, I thought, and this became the first item on my future guilt list.

She was given medication to control the swelling in her head. Had to continue the pills for the epileptic seizures, plus a powder to protect her stomach. I had listed them all, and looked up what they all did. When the nurse brought them, in the morning and evening, I put a dash next to the names. I think I believed I still had control over *something*, that way.

Julian slept a lot and, even in the daytime, there were moments when she was no longer cognizant. I saw it in her eyes. I could see when she saw me and when she didn't. I talked to her and read to her from *Dance Dance Dance* by Murakami, her favourite writer. While she was sleeping, I looked for another book because I had the impression that she could no longer follow the story.

On the sixth day, she had to go under the scanner one last time.

The next day was December 9, 2017 and we had been together for seven years. On Facebook I wrote:

Today, 7 years ago, I met the most wonderful woman I have ever known.

7 years of unconditional love
7 years of saying 'yes' to new adventures
7 years of trying to live the life we imagine
7 years of magic
7 years of joy when I see her face
7 years of faith in our madness
7 years of curiosity and dreams
And still my most favourite human being in the whole world.

Let's add another 50 years!

Two hours later I was told that radiotherapy was pointless and that she only had three months to live. She had more than fifty tumours. In her brain, around her heart, and on her bones. A total destruction of that beautiful body.

=

Whatever you do, you must not move, start a relationship, or buy a pet after your partner dies. It's in all the books I've read about grief. The dog and the relationship don't even occur to me, and I don't own a house. I search for what I want, and like in the films, I watch myself stepping from one scene into the next. Slipping from one personality into another. I take what feels good, leaving any unnecessary and negative baggage behind. I have never thought of myself as someone trailing round insurmountable baggage. It took me a long time to get over my divorce from Jeroen emotionally, but I tied up everything neatly. Now, I have lived the worst nightmare I could imagine and I can never return to any version of myself I have ever been. My life will never be a hundred percent okay again.

When Julian fell ill, I felt myself disintegrating along with her; when she died, I became a void that was unable to be filled. Now, every person in my path leaves an imprint that I either take with me or shake off. They write about being reborn when someone dies, but I dispute this. There is no new beginning, no blank page. It's embroidering in a vacuum where the horror always shines through.

We all look for meaning in tragedy. 'Man's main concern is not to gain pleasure or avoid pain, but rather to see a meaning in his life,' wrote Austrian psychologist Viktor Frankl. It's not the pain and sorrow, but the sense of uselessness that makes me long for death. Because, why bother if nothing matters anymore? Still, I intuitively feel that the ability to move forwards depends on the goals I set for myself. Or, try to set. I follow Frankl who says, 'There is nothing in the world that would so effectively help one to survive even the worst conditions as the knowledge that there is meaning in one's life.' Frankl survived three concentration camps, so he knows what he's talking about, I guess. Nietzsche also agrees: 'He who has a *why* to live for can bear almost any *how*.' Julian was a large part of my 'meaning' and the sum of the two of us worked towards a greater – at least for us – purpose. When she stopped breathing, the life I loved so much came to a halt. And, yet I want to continue our work. That, I feel, is the key.

I look for meaning, even though I know it only exists in my head. After all, isn't everything a construct? An illusion upon which to pin our own goals? Like big, shiny baubles in a Christmas tree? A distorted reality, but my reality nevertheless? 'Ultimately, man should not ask what the meaning of his life is, but rather he must recognise that it is he who is asked.' Again, Frankl. Reinventing myself is the only solution.

In the five months since her death, I've lectured, written, talked, listened, and read a lot. Researchers at Radboud University in Nijmegen have recently discovered that emotional memories are stored differently than everyday memories. The latter are shifted into long-term memory over time. 'In addition, the role of the hippocampus becomes smaller and the role of the cerebral cortex increases. Because of this reorganisation of the neural network, such everyday memories lose their sharpness and detail in the new "memory trail".' Emotional events, however, resist the memory transfer from hippocampus to cerebral cortex and thus follow a different neurological pathway.

My wife is dead and I am producing new memories, but I will always see her deteriorate, in detail. That's what this means … .

*All I wanted to do was hide. I took
comfort in sadistically drowning paper
in the blackest of black ink, leaving
minimal white space for the strange
scenarios and characters that seemed to
mysteriously well up inside of me.*

In conversation with Betty Black
Et Alors? Magazine

THE DIAGNOSIS GAVE HER THREE MONTHS
to live. But, the doctor also came up with
a solution that actually wasn't one. They
could stretch out her life for another
twenty years, but she would never leave
the hospital again. First, radiotherapy.
Her head would sustain third-degree
burns. But, there was an ointment for
that, a helpful nurse said. After the
radiotherapy, treatment would follow for
the tumours surrounding her heart, and
then for the tumours that surrounded her
bones. The big problem was that she
would be in pain. And, also, that they
could not perform these three different
therapies at the same time. First, number
one, while the rest continued to grow.
Then number two. And so on. In the
meantime, the growth was temporarily

halted, but subsequently given free rein.
Her memory would never be what it was.
It would only be a temporary halt, but
with no improvement. Twenty years in a
hospital bed with a consciousness that's
switched off half the time. It was a surreal
proposition.

'What do you want me to do?' she asked.

'I can't tell you,' I said. 'But whatever you choose, I will
never leave you. Even if I have to live in a hospital room for
twenty years.'

I meant it. Without a second's hesitation.

What would have happened if she had chosen those twenty
years? Our world would be a white box. A hospital room
with, hopefully, a window. Julian in the middle of a large bed
with side rails. They are called safety rails. They were needed
from the first night, as she'd unwittingly wriggled to the edge
of the bed. To the side where I was sleeping, on a camping
cot, a metre below. Chances were, she'd fall out of bed.

When I was sitting or lying on her bed, I lowered them.
As soon as I got up, I put them back up. 'All aboard!' I'd say.
It made her smile. Even though I said it more than ten times
a day.

Julian considered the twenty years, but the prospect of a
lot of pain, with no possibility of an active life, is what made
the difference.

I could have had her with me for another 20 years, I think
now, and I wonder if I should have convinced her. Whichever
way the scenario is written, it makes me feel selfish. I could

have kept her with me for all these years, but she would be in pain. And what is a life consisting of twenty years imprisonment, surrounded by medicinal smells, and totally dependent? At least in this story I get another life. But, what kind of life? My head has become a tiny space in which past and present fight for priority. In terms of quality of life, it would not have made much difference.

=

Christopher Isherwood estimated that he'd had 'somewhere around four hundred' bedpartners when he met Don Bachardy in 1952. The writer of *Mr. Norris Changes Trains* and *A Single Man* was forty-eight at the time. Bachardy was eighteen. The age gap raised many eyebrows, and Bachardy was seen as a kind of sexworker. Despite their ages, and challenges like infidelity, debauchery, and power games, they stayed together for thirty-four years and became a well-known and recognised couple within the Hollywood community.

Encouraged by Isherwood, Bachardy became a competent portraitist who painted the movie stars in their circle of friends. They called themselves complementary: a writer and a visual artist. 'We were both watchers,' Bachardy said in an interview. 'I record the way people look, Chris described the way they behaved.' In *The Animals: Love Letters Between Christopher Isherwood and Don Bachardy*, you can read how they defied convention by publicly living as a gay couple. In romantic letters, the couple create a loving account of an extraordinary and symbiotic relationship.

When Isherwood died in 1986, Bachardy read his diaries. For six months he read his way back in time to the moment they met. 'It was my way of keeping him alive,' he said. 'I could hear his voice in every sentence, and there were messages he left for me in his more recent volumes, since he was so concerned about leaving me alone.'

Literature expert Peter Conrad noted in an article in The Guardian that, during the interview with Bachardy, he imagined himself in Isherwood's company. Bachardy had taken on the same wiry body, the same accent, and the same piercing look. When he shared his findings with Bachardy, the latter took it as a compliment. Conrad continues, 'Love never dies, because loved ones stay alive in the books they have written or the portraits made of them. In this case there is an additional bonus: Bachardy's gift for mimicry has transformed him, almost miraculously, into Isherwood reincarnated.'

=

Sometimes I provoke my own grief. I test how far it can pull me across the line, and how resilient I am. I try to find out if it could get any worse. It can always get worse. There is a list in my head of heartrending moments, and that inventory shows up at the most unexpected times. All those moments pass before my eyes, one by one - like scenes from a film. One event is disguised as a small animal that keeps scratching back and forth in the same spot, with its hard little claws, another dropped on top of me one night like a veritable panic monster. I deliberately add details. Dot by dot, in living colour. Unstoppable, until I go down.

My list includes: her facial expression when I reveal the diagnosis. Her soft ouch, when her foot gets stuck in the bed rail, is on it. Her look of unwavering trust, and my realisation that my strong wife has become completely dependent on me. The moment she wonders why she can't hold her fork properly. And, one of the worst on the list: the doctor warning me, a week before her death, to be careful (even more careful) when I turn her over in bed. Because she could break. When the list has laid its full weight on me, so vivid that all the oxygen is sucked out of me, I wonder how much more I can take. But, I notice there's always room for something else.

I am angry, sad, disappointed, but I also notice there's a kind of fearlessness in the making. Because, every time I fall, I get up again, straighten myself up, and brush myself off. I let it fully sink in that I have lived my worst nightmare. The greatest horror I could possibly imagine. But, each time, I get back up, look life straight in the eye, and say out loud, 'Bring it on!'

I know that if I want to learn how to live with this, fear is a luxury I can no longer afford. Courage is fear in motion.

THE DAY OF THAT FATAL DIAGNOSIS, THE SUN WAS SHINING IN
a fresh, bright blue sky. I stood in front of the window,
watching life go by in the street. One woman was sweeping
her front path, another was lifting her child out of the car,
an elderly couple walked hand in hand. He was carrying the
shopping bags. I heard the nurses laugh in the hall. They
were busy decorating a Christmas tree.

Where were you happiest, I once asked Julian. Happiness
sometimes needs benchmarks. Happy. Happier. Happiest.

Christmas Day 2016, she'd said. New York, three months
after her surgery. A walk in the snow. We saw The Muppet
Christmas Carol, holding hands at the Roxy Hotel cinema.
Followed by almond-milk hot chocolate on a bench in Bryant
Park, with a view of the Christmas tree.

'All the clichés in one pile,' she said.

'Nice, huh?' I said.

I loved Christmas. My wife didn't, but she said the look
on my face made up for everything.

I reflected that, from this moment on, I would never again

be able to look at a Christmas tree with an open mind. In the hallway, the nurse was fixing a wooden Santa on the door.

'I will try not to die on Christmas Day,' she said, a few days later.

'In a way, you're lucky,' said the doctor, 'She's not going to feel anything: all her bodily functions will shut down and she will completely lose her memory. She will not feel any pain and, fortunately, she won't realise it.'

'Yes, we are very lucky,' I said.

He stared at me blankly.

He asked if I was going to tell her. Of course I was going to tell her. However, I lied and told her she still had six months. I don't know why, but it seemed important to say six instead of three. She cried, I cried. The first thing she said was that she was so sorry she had to leave me. And she apologised for all the grief she would cause me.

'I won't go blind, will I?' she asked sometime later.

'No, not blind. Fortunately.'

Another lie. With luck, she would no longer realise it.

'How am I going to die?' she asked the doctor.

He told her she would go to sleep and gently slip into a coma. When the time came, they would see if they could proceed with euthanasia.

Every time she got tired, she became afraid of falling asleep. I talked until I couldn't go on anymore, and then put on some music or a film. Once, we stayed awake for more than 40 hours. Until she forgot why she had to stay awake and fell asleep, exhausted. When I noticed her getting tired, I would kiss her and say she was the best thing that ever happened to me. Just to be sure.

=

Renate remains tireless in her reassurances. I can't count the times I've asked her if I really couldn't have done any more.

'No,' she says. 'I saw her at your wedding in Antwerp at the end of October, and two months later she was almost gone. You couldn't have done anything.'

Didn't I poison her with all those drugs? She shakes her head again. The doctor had given her the lowest dose of morphine, and when I talked to him about her headache, he slowly increased the dose. That was two weeks before she died. 'People use heroin and don't die,' says Renate. 'The dose just wasn't strong enough to die from it.' According to her, there was nothing I could have done. Nothing I could have done better. But, I, myself have forgotten.

'Are we talking enough?' Julian had asked me twice in the first week after her diagnosis. Those words have dug their claws into my mind. They return, and sadden me more each day. It's the greatest guilt I carry after her death. Maybe she had forgotten that we'd talked an hour earlier. But, maybe not. The problem is, my memory is empty. I remember thinking: 'I have to do this right'. I was looking for ways to say something without upsetting her. Sometimes, I wonder whether I should have better recognised, and made use of, the moments when she was lucid. But, maybe I did. I don't know anymore.

When someone is dying, you must only answer the questions he or she is asking, I recently read. Because, that's the only information they can handle. So, definitely don't elaborate. This theory is – occasionally – a comfort.

Julian was really good at pep talks, when I had doubts about the quality of my work. When I was worried. Within a second she came up with a positive lecture that immediately put me in a different mood.

I was the opposite. When something was bothering her, I listened and asked questions. She once told me that she, too, needed that kind of a stimulating sermon from time to time. I did try, but failed miserably.

Now I sometimes think that, had I been the one lying there, she would have guided me effortlessly. That she would have talked me through it. Maybe I did, too. Maybe, this time, it worked. It remains an elusive part of my memory.

I'm working hard on those guilty feelings. These are stories I tell myself that I know I will have to let go of someday, if I want to make even the slightest progress. Dealing with something as overwhelming as the steep decline towards death, we had been left to ourselves. I did what I could, I often hear myself say, while a little voice screams, 'Not good enough!' through it. But, I'm trying to see it for what it is. A voice. And many stories.

Often grief is considered inappropriate, as if it has a certain expiration date after which you have to get on with it.

In conversation with Jonathan Kemp
Et Alors? Magazine

THE THOUGHT OF SUICIDE QUICKLY AROSE.

'May I come with you?' I asked her.

'No,' she said, after a long pause. 'Because, what if we can't find each other? What if it turns out not to be true?'

Once an astrologer had told us that we were connected to each other. That we had met each other many times, in other lifetimes. I didn't know if it was true, but I'll believe anything as long as it's a good story.

In all our years together, we both felt that there was 'something.' I called it *something*, she called it *universe*. Something that guided us, that gave us a sign if we were on the right track. In practical terms, it often happened that when we started a new project, we suddenly encountered the right people who could give it a push forward. 'A sign that we're on the right track,' we would say. But, the brain automatically searches for answers. We were probably just asking the right questions.

'Don't,' she finally said.

Disappointed, I promised. 'But, I think we *will* find each

other again,' I said. 'To me, every minute will seem like a lifetime, but to you it will feel like I just went to the toilet.'

'How do you know?' she asked.

'No idea. But, that's how it feels right now.'

She looked at me doubtfully and fell back to sleep.

=

Six months after her death, an email arrives asking if I'd like to give a lecture series in New York. In exchange for the lectures, I get a room for a month. I want to stay longer, but I don't really have the money.

'Do it anyway,' says Renate. 'Think of it as an investment in your future.'

So, I book the full three months that my visa allows me to stay. I repack all my things, which still fit in one suitcase. A life in free fall.

Drowsily, I stand in line for those who get to decide whether I can enter their country. Sleepy and nervous, as I always am around people in uniform.

'Why such a funny look on your face?' asks the man behind the desk.

'I wasn't aware of it,' I say.

'Okay,' he says, stamping my passport. 'Welcome to the United States.'

New York is just as big, busy, and loud as it was when I was there with Julian, but now the city makes me feel invisible in a way I'd never experienced before.

Just a year ago, we were giving interviews every day, and people called us to meet. Now I stagger through the streets, wondering if I will ever be able to undo that chilling loneliness.

'You can always come back,' my mother and Renate say on the phone. 'You don't have to do this,' says Marscha, my editor. But I feel like I will never make any progress if I go back now. I want to persevere and keep in mind the words of psychotherapist Thomas Moore: 'You can turn humiliation into courage, and fear into a love for that little bit of life that is still inside you.' It's tempting to look at everything one-dimensionally: she's dead and my life is over. So, how do I turn this around? It feels as unnatural as it would for a motorcyclist to let his body go down into the bend, rather than intuitively lean the other way. I lean into my grief and loneliness, and I will only notice when my face hits the concrete.

Just like in Antwerp, I roam from one lodging to another in New York. Sometimes my financial condition sends me into rooms long past their prime; where I am one of the few people on the subway at night. Where I then have to walk five blocks through dimly lit streets, and where, every night, I get a slight panic attack when the key doesn't properly fit. The desolate streets are too vast, too quiet, and too reflective of my own feeling that I'm disappearing.

During the day, in the absence of any energy, I rely on the city's electricity. The constant murmur of cars, of voices, the sirens, and the people who, always in a hurry, slalom around every obstacle. Sometimes I am that obstacle, but usually I keep up with the pace. You walk like a New Yorker, says an acquaintance, a local. And I see it as a compliment. Forward, and without compromise.

As time goes by, we are expanding our capacity. We continue to add various elements and new points of view to our personality, until we are like a bunch of grapes.

In conversation with Pyuupiru
Et Alors? Magazine

AFTER THE DIAGNOSIS I DID WHAT I DO BEST: I STARTED organising. Organising meant that there was room for change. Anything was better than watching the love of my life die. As long as I had something to do, perhaps the last few months wouldn't be a total disaster. Why do we keep on kidding ourselves? From hoping for a treatment that could possibly cure her, I seamlessly transitioned into end-of-life care. Because I had to keep myself strong.

Don't cry, she had said after the diagnosis, when I needed to hold on to the wall, time and again, to keep from collapsing. Since then, I had banished all tears, and sometimes stood in the hallway hyperventilating because I wanted her wish to take precedence over my emotions. I waited for her to go to sleep, and then tiptoed into the small bathroom where I lowered myself to the floor between the shower and the toilet. I pushed my nails into my body, to feel a different kind of pain, and opened my mouth in a silent scream. If I stepped back into the room and she turned out to be awake, I always said something trivial – 'So nice that the sun is shining' or 'I hope my mother will bring us some pears,' and the like. As if I could defuse the horror of the situation by letting life carry on.

I never found out why she didn't want me to cry. She couldn't tell me that. I can imagine that, when you know you are dying, you don't particularly feel like seeing people cry around you all the time. Or, maybe it was because it made her cry too. Or, because she wanted to tell herself that I was fine. But, it was something that would bother me later. Did she realise how devastated I actually was? Wouldn't she think I was taking it all too lightly? Whatever I did, and no matter how well I tried to do it, it was never enough.

With the exception of 'don't cry,' most of the time my wife remained her sweet and empathetic self. I was the one she worried about, not herself. What I would do, if I could ever be happy again. How I had to go through all the worries with her.

One night she couldn't sleep, and I lay down next to her. I talked about our wedding project, and what a strange feeling it was that we weren't going to finish it. When we had been so sure that the project needed to be realised.

'Looks like it wasn't meant to be,' she said. 'Or, maybe something else has to take its place. But, this clearly wasn't it.'

'But, why you, and not me?'

She looked at me and I could see in her eyes that we were running out of time, that her brain was slowly sinking again.

'Because you can do this,' she said. After that it went quiet.

We were able to stay in the hospital for a few more days but, as there was nothing more they could do for her, we had to leave. Since we couldn't return to Spain either, I was looking for options in the surrounding area. The idea had been to take her to a hospice that provided end-of-life care, but I couldn't find a single place that would let me stay with her full-time. My mother, from whom I had inherited my determination, arranged for a hospital bed to be delivered to her home three days later. She called the village doctor, who had been the first to examine Julian, and who agreed to supervise the pain medication. She had me sign the papers allowing the hospital to waive responsibility.

At the hospital they advised against taking her home, as she could potentially become very aggressive. I said these were concerns for the future, and there was no way I was going to leave her alone.

Julian followed all the complications and looked at me with eyes that were often unreadable. After the diagnosis, her voice had grown weaker and she was losing her mobility at lightning speed. It was as if she had been waiting for permission to let go.

'Go ahead,' I said, caressing her face, 'We're going home.'

The last days at the hospital were no different than before, but a storm raged inside me. Everything had become unreal now that her unending absence had come into my purview. I barely left the room, for fear that something would happen in the meantime. Because, she might panic if I wasn't there when she woke up. I had no idea what the hospital looked like outside of this room and hallway.

When she fell asleep, I walked barefoot to the doctor's office. Down a hallway with coughing people, all of them pale and hairless. I stared at the ground. My toenails were brightly painted. A vestige from another life, only weeks earlier. Julian sitting next to me on the couch with my foot in her hand.

'It's winter, so we're going to do some cheerful little nails,' she'd said, waving around the bottle of pink nail varnish.

'You are so gay!' I laughed.

By now, the varnish was flaking.

A daily trip from her room to the doctor's office.

'Are you sure?' I asked him for the umpteenth time. Each time, he patiently pulled out the scans. The only way I could look inside that beautiful, but hostile, body. Numerous white spots in her skull. Clusters around her heart. Large white circles on her bones. The last scan was the worst. The expanse of her skeleton. She had turned her right foot slightly inward. Her shoulders were hunched, her head turned a bit to the side and down. I saw the tumours on the bones in her hands, her legs, her face. My wife was being devoured from the inside, and I could tell from her posture that she knew.

I asked the doctor to repeat it in English. Maybe I had missed something in French. But, a second doctor and a third also said the same. There was absolutely nothing that could be done.

Exhausted, I walked back down the hall to the room and, with dirty feet, I crawled into bed with her.

=

David Wojnarowicz is one of my favourite artists. Three weeks before my wife died, I received an announcement in my inbox of a retrospective exhibition in New York. It was the beginning of January; the exhibition ran until the end of October and I already knew, even then, that I would need to go and mourn there. What I also knew was that there would be no certain outcome. If there's one city where you might jump out of the window through sheer loneliness, it's New York.

The word 'alone' is composed of all + one. You alone, without an other. And, while you can feel lonely anywhere, there is a loneliness in New York which is devastating. The kind of loneliness that burrows inside my mind, making me feel like I'll never be able to shake it off again. It stays close beside me. Even in company, when every face that surrounds me is not hers.

I wish I could capture that feeling and put it in a box. That way, I could make it manageable. Loneliness forces you to think about what is keeping you in this world. And whether you still want to be here. Loneliness doesn't go away because you fight it. It can only be exorcised, by being personal with someone. Getting recognition of your existence by being heard. I am not lonely as such, but I am lonely without her. Sometimes, so badly that it becomes physical. Like a cold hand pressing down on my chest, until I feel like I'm drowning. Loneliness is not fatal. That's too bad.

You see the lonely everywhere. Their pleading eyes and their tendency to shrink away, while longing to be seen. The flash of envy that passes over their faces when a couple walks by, hands intertwined. 'Loneliness leads people to make each other even lonelier,' wrote Dimitri Verhulst.

I feel both pity and compassion for them, for the lonely ones, but at the same time I feel a huge loathing for them, being so close on my heels. Because, I could join their ranks at any time if I'm not paying attention, if I should lose sight of my protective layer for a moment. Before you know it, like Catherine Deneuve in *Repulsion*, I'll be madly trying to crawl away from the hands grabbing for me out of the walls.

'Are you ashamed of your loneliness?' asks Renate, and I notice that I have very little left to be ashamed of. However, it's not social isolation I'm sinking deeper and deeper into, and I remind myself of this fundamental difference. I try to accept loneliness for what it is. Part of my grief, and not, as I had previously thought, an indication of depression or fear. The fear of loneliness can make us do anything. We accept partners who are not our equals and we throw ourselves into promiscuity to give our body some respite, by pressing another body against it. My body is unaware of her death, and I have to suppress the urge to let many others take her place. Albeit nothing more than a fleeting fantasy .

I develop a relationship with my body that I've never had before. When something goes wrong, I either stop breathing or I breathe too much; I run into things, or I have to hold on to something to keep from falling. My body has become a loose cannon, but I humour it like I would a recalcitrant animal and learn to be forbearing. I recognise the warning signs, and try to decipher their symbolism.

=

'Everything I make, I make for Peter,' said artist David Wojnarowicz.

He met Peter Hujar, twenty years his senior and already an established photographer, in New York in 1980, at a time when the AIDS crisis was raging through America. Entire communities were wiped out and the government did nothing. According to the World Health Organization, thirty-nine million people worldwide died of AIDS. 76.1 million people became infected. Even then, president Ronald Reagan refused to take preventative measures such as educating people about the disease, the distribution of condoms, funding research to develop medications, or making testing available. It wasn't until five years after the outbreak of the epidemic, that he mentioned the disease for the first time in a public speech.

Peter Hujar was the one who gave Wojnarowicz shelter after a lifetime of abuse, and who managed to help him get off heroin. He was the first person to take his artwork seriously.

Hujar was infected with AIDS, and died seven years after they met. It was a slow and painful death, due to lack of medication and medical support. Wojnarowicz wrote about Hujar's illness in his diaries. About all the desperate attempts they made to cure him. In one passage, he describes how they went to a clinic on Long Island together, where they discovered that the doctor was injecting patients with human faeces as an experiment.

When Hujar is dying, Wojnarowicz takes his Super 8 camera and films his lover, best friend and father figure. The black-and-white images show the photographer in a hospital bed. Emaciated. There are images of his hands, of his feet.

In the spring of 1988, Wojnarowicz, too, was diagnosed with AIDS, a few months after Hujar's death. His ensuing work is permeated with political and social activism. It documents a period of despair, which he translates into timeless images of sex, spirituality, love, and loss. He uses every medium he could to express what he had to say. He was a photographer, musician, filmmaker, painter, poet, writer, and speaker. The absence of any kind of commerciality makes his work both uninhibited and merciless. He channelled the loss of his partner into an adamant plea for everyone confronted by AIDS. It's an indictment of the US government for ignoring the epidemic, and doing nothing to address one of the greatest crises of the twentieth century. Wojnarowicz's work appealed to thousands of people. Decades after his death, his passionate activism still remains a source of inspiration to many.

He died in 1992, at the age of thirty-seven. His retrospective, *History Keeps Me Awake at Night*, is running at the Whitney Museum. His work gives me strength and, like a junkie, I visit the exhibition four times.

=

Every dream starts with a 'What if?' We were not able to realise one of our ultimate dreams, but it remains stuck in my head. Although it's impossible to accurately measure such things, according to the American Coalition for the Homeless, 20 percent of homeless youths are either gay or trans. In Great Britain the estimate is around 25 percent. Many of them have been kicked out by their parents because of their sexual orientation, and have little or no future prospects. Often, they end up going into sexwork just to survive.

Our dream started out relatively small: wouldn't it be great if we could open a shelter? Start with one, and who knows where it might lead. This dream drove our imagination in all kinds of directions, and acquired more layers and dimensions over the years. We were no strangers to megalomania, and towards the end of her life we dreamed of purchasing one of those abandoned American ghost towns, and then building a community, where homeless LGBTQ+ youngsters could be cared for and given housing. We'd grow our own fruit and vegetables and independently supply our own water and electricity. We would have a library, filled with all the books about the history of gay culture and all the giants upon whose shoulders we now stand, in order to carry on living. A movie theatre would chart the evolution of gay cinema. Motivational speakers from all over the world would come and give lectures and workshops, to give those kids a glimpse of all the possibilities they do have. There would be individual sessions to explore what their personal interests were, and how they could move forwards with them. Once we'd built up their strength, then they would be ready to go back out into the world, with a user's manual for life. It was something we would tinker with for hours, and each time a new brick was added.

Julian loved working on this plan, and had created a folder on her computer with ideas, thoughts, and the practicalities. With her background, she loved to examine whether something like this would be structurally feasible.

Every once in a while, I flip through her notes, and each time I do I feel the enthusiasm bubble up inside again. Knowing us, we would definitely have tried to get this project underway. But, what am I capable of alone?

I decided to look at the past in order to understand the future.

In conversation with Matthijs Holland
Et Alors? Magazine

AT NIGHT, AND WHENEVER SHE SLEPT, I READ, LOOKING FOR helpful hints. How to deal with her. How to deal with a brain that's falling apart, deteriorating at breakneck speed. A brain that turned my sharp, intelligent, funny wife into a creature that looked at me helplessly and soundlessly. How to deal with someone who was dying, but who just turned 40 and who loved life so much. Repetition is important, I read. Talking is important. It creates neurological pathways in the brain. Compare it to a forest trail which becomes easier to follow over time. Do I have that time, I wondered? And what should I say? What are the most important words you can say to the love of your life? For the first time in seven years, I didn't know how to talk to her. I was so afraid of doing something wrong, saying something wrong. Keep it simple, I thought. And do it fast.

I will always love you.
I will never forget you.
You are in my heart forever.
I will never leave you.

I spoke these lines for six weeks. One after the other. In the same order. I put her hand on my cheek and gazed at her. I built a path from my heart to her damaged brain and hoped it would last.

=

New York has me breathing again. The amount of noise, galleries, and restaurants is comforting. As if the proximity of possibility, even if I sometimes don't participate in it for days, appeases the urgency.

The same CD has been playing for weeks at the Colombian coffee bar round the corner. Something that would drive me up the walls in any other circumstance, but which now gives me an uncanny sense of stability. The two women behind the counter at Roth Bar make me laugh out loud, with their pretend bickering which gets funnier and funnier as their audience grows. They call me sweetie, and remember I don't want an egg on my avocado toast. I want to hug them with gratitude, but then I'd have to explain why, and I want to carry on feeling like everyone else who sits at their counter.

Often, I dawdle in front of one of the dozens of shop windows promoting fortune-tellers, tarot readers, and mediums. Hollow-eyed, and desperately wanting a manual for the future. But, I dare not enter. Will I still be able to handle life if someone tells me it's going to get even worse? I opt for a safe middle ground, and buy a bag of fortune cookies in Chinatown.

'Your dreams will come true.' 'You will live long enough to read many fortune cookies.' 'You enjoy Chinese food.' I line up the good fortunes on my nightstand. I throw away the more ambiguous statements – too confusing. I put the broken cookies in a bowl in the living room, where my housemate, a man with a strong appetite for varied women, eats them for breakfast.

In 2017, a man who wrote fortune cookie quotes for thirty years left the trade. Writer's block, he stated in Time.

I am greeted with kisses at the Indian restaurant whose owner had read our first New York article aloud. It has been a year since we were here, but apparently he has a phenomenal memory. First kisses, then wet-eyed hugs when I answer their questions about why Julian isn't here. My lunch is on the house. With dessert to go, and a firm promise made to return.

Food and mourning. It's a wonderful combination. 'Call me if there's anything I can do,' I often hear. But, when you are grieving you don't call, because you don't know what someone might be able do for you. It's only when they are at your door with food that you realise what you wanted to ask for. It moves me, time and again, that returning to the essence. So, I eat. I nourish my body with love, with good intentions, and with the strength of someone else. Because, you have to start somewhere.

In New York, Siri Hustvedt takes me out to dinner. After our first meeting, two years ago, she had kept in touch and regularly enquired how Julian, and later I, was doing. Now, she offers me the beautiful thought that the people you meet become an expansion of your 'self.' Other people help you to grow, like stacked building blocks. She says that, since we met, Julian and I have become an extension of herself, and she of us. And that she hopes that we'll become good friends. It's one of those times when I bow my head in surrender to everything I'm grateful for. I realise I need to rid myself of the guilty feeling that every beautiful moment which comes my way is a denial of the horror of her death.

That a lotus grows out of the mud doesn't mean the mud should be glorified.

Art gives a more added value to my life
than religion. I don't need to listen to a
human invention. I'd rather listen to
myself in everything that I do.

In conversation with Faryda Moumouh
Et Alors? Magazine

OLIVER SACKS' *THE MAN WHO MISTOOK HIS WIFE FOR A HAT*
was on my mother's bookshelf. It had a deep impact on me
as a teenager. Such an impact, even, that years later I still
occasionally relayed one of the stories. In the story in question, the neurologist describes the condition of one of his
patients: a Functional Neurological Disorder where the
woman was only able to move her limbs when she looked at
them – her brain had stopped transmitting the signal otherwise. When the doctor asked her to bend her leg, the woman
said she needed to find it first. Once her eyes found her leg,
then she could move it. I got goosebumps every time I told
the story. The concept that your brain has so much power
that it can involuntarily influence your motor skills and
behaviour was (and still is) something that terrifies me.

During the long nights on the camp bed, under the flimsy
blanket, I often thought I was losing my mind. I once read a
story by Guy de Maupassant that frightened me similarly. In
the story, a woman suddenly displays strange traits. She
forgets things, quarrels, occasionally faints, and throws

dishes around. One of the witnesses notices that one of her eyes is sometimes slightly larger than the other. The woman dies young, and nobody knows why. De Maupassant gives a brief explanation: the woman had a brain tumour, but at the time medical science was not adequately equipped to detect it.

In Paris, Julian had become dizzy. She had a headache – 'Like there's something in my head that needs to get out' – and said it seemed like 'everything was upside down.' I didn't realise at the time that our eyes see everything upside down, and our brains then turn what we see the right way up. Her brain could no longer do this. What I did realise, in that cold hospital room, was that my wife was going through one of my worst nightmares.

Two literary descriptions of a medical condition that I felt were the most sinister possible threats to life, and my wife had this. No other form of cancer, no, just the one I knew about. I thought I was going crazy.

Elon Musk once said in an interview that he is convinced we're living in a computer simulation. That reality is only in our heads. He argued that our evolutionary forerunners had designed a game and are playing it now to control us. I find Musk intriguing. Whenever he proposes something new, everyone screams that he's crazy and that it will never work. When it does work, praise is heaped on him and he is called a visionary. However, the idea of a simulated reality is not new. In the seventeenth century Descartes spoke about his thought experiment brain in a vat. The theory was as follows: our brains are floating in a container of fluid and our neurons are connected to a machine that simulates a visual reality.

Our brains are fed images, sound, reality, truth, conscious-ness, and knowledge, and therefore have the same experience as if they were in a physical body. In 1999, the Wachowskis based the film The Matrix on this theory; where Neo has to choose between the blue pill and the red one. Does he want to experience reality, or will he choose to continue living the illusion?

However, Musk, the man who wants to put the first humans on Mars by 2025, has an explanation for this too. During a live interview at the Recode technology conference, the founder of Tesla and SpaceX said: 'The strongest argu-ment for us being in a simulation probably is the following. Forty years ago, we had Pong. Like, two rectangles and a dot. That was what games were. Now, 40 years later, we have photorealistic, 3D simulations with millions of people play-ing simultaneously, and it's getting better every year. Soon, we'll have virtual reality, augmented reality. If you assume any rate of improvement at all, then the games will become indistinguishable from reality, even if that rate of advance-ment drops by a thousand from what it is now.' He added that we are likely to already be in that future now, and that the odds that our reality is the original is one in billions.

These kinds of thought experiments can run wild when the love of your life is dying and you're stuck in a 100 square foot space. Since our arrival I had barely left the room, and it seemed as if the world consisted of a cube surrounded by nothing but emptiness. Here, my thoughts were bouncing between one wall and the other. 'Don't worry,' said Jeroen when I later expressed my suspicions. 'You are here. For real.' But, of course he would say that. After all, he was in this same reality as I was. Which I could have created as my reality. He couldn't have said otherwise.

=

Today I'm turning forty-five. I remember my first birthday living in Spain. The house was a mess from renovations, but Julian insisted that we celebrate on our roof terrace. She had put up bunting, and bought an oversized cupcake. And fifteen candles that spelled out 'Feliz Cumpleaños.' Only the 'Feli' fitted, and I can still see her coming up the stairs, singing loudly, in a striped t-shirt, her hand in front of the candles to protect them from the wind. Even so, everything got covered in candle wax, but she picked it all off the cake before feeding me mouthfuls of it.

We were going to grow old together. Time and age play no part in forever. Only when it stops will it catch up with you, in record time. Time is no longer linear. It's spinning in circles, and I'm trying like crazy to create a number of resting points. Points where I can pick things up and leave other things behind. In the first five years of our relationship, we lived as if time did not exist. Grown-ups, those were the others, the ones living in that other, parallel world that was based on time, and where all kinds of serious things went on. We had a built-in urge to play. And, disregarding the concept of time was part of that. We had our deadlines, but they were the only things that were fixed. Apart from that, we got up and went to sleep when it suited us. We woke each other up in the middle of the night, got in the car and drove to Madrid. To have breakfast there in the morning, at a coffee bar where the clock said eight a.m. but to us it might as well have been four in the afternoon. We wandered through cities and got lost on purpose. Time stretched, walked with us, caught up or left us behind. But, we were not aware of it. We were so adept at living and consumed those seven years as if they were thirty.

Love gives you the illusion of immortality. Faith in the world becomes so all-encompassing that death seems like an invention which only happens to other people.

I have watched Death approach and devour. He was not gentle. In the six weeks between diagnosis and death, the crushing reality was maddening, and left me with an insight into the concept of time that I will never be able to shake off. Time was not on our side, and the world was not as beautiful and inviting as I had always thought.

You can count yourself lucky, I hear around me, you have known a love that most of us will never experience. 'It's better to have loved and lost than never to have loved at all,' wrote Alfred Lord Tennyson, and everyone accepts it as true. Perhaps I'll be able to respond to this in a year. Today I am still staring straight ahead, powerless, while loneliness digs its way in.

It takes time, it is said and written. But, it is precisely this abundance of time that oppresses me. I think about my family and the strong line of women I come from. My grand-mother is in her nineties, and still rides her bike every day. My mother is over seventy, yet acts as if she's twenty. When I consider all those years potentially stretching out ahead of me, time becomes an scary prospect. If I have those same genes, eventually I'll have been around for more than twice as long as I've lived till now. The thought of having to spend another fifty years without Julian terrifies me.

Love is something that everyone can relate to.

In conversation with Rhys Chapman
Et Alors? Magazine

I SENT EMAILS ABOUT THE DIAGNOSIS TO JEROEN, RENATE, all our friends, and hers. I knew that, unless I did that, I would never accept it. By announcing it, it became true. However, the emails were not enough. I wanted to pause people's lives, just like ours had been, albeit just for a moment. On Facebook someone was raging about some politician. Another person claimed to be 'devastated' by a traffic fine.

'The love of my life is dying,' I wrote on my profile. Life was paused. Just for a moment.

Everyone I messaged was prepared to get in their cars and drive. I waited for Julian to have a moment of clarity, to ask her if she wanted visitors. She thought about it for a long time, then decided it was not a good idea. She very much wanted to see all our friends one last time, but, 'I will become mentally impaired. It's bad enough that you will have to witness that.'

However, Jeroen and his wife Nikkie cleared their diaries, and decided to stay with me as long as I wanted. 'You will

254 | FLEUR PIERETS

need help, too,' said Jeroen. That settled it. Renate, too, made plans to come to France. Despite my protestations that I was perfectly capable of handling everything on my own, I was relieved and grateful to know that they were on their way.

After my Facebook post I was flooded with messages. People asked for more information. I gave them all the details. Every message was proof of our new reality. Friends wrote letters to her and I told them she could no longer read them, but I would read them to her. I asked her if she wanted me to do that. She nodded. Julian never imagined there were so many people who loved her, and after a few letters she was crying so hard she nearly choked. I stopped reading them and did not bring it up again. I'm not sure if she had forgotten or if she no longer wanted it, but I didn't propose it again. Her parents, too, got in touch. Six years earlier Julian had broken off contact and, since that time they had not communicated at all. I said her parents wanted to see her and asked how she felt about that. She refused, and said that she had never regretted her decision. I was relieved that I had still been able to ask her such an important question.

Hundreds of people sent me strength and love. If, decades ago, I would have found myself all alone in a hospital room without any outside contact, I was now supported virtually, by a Facebook community of friends, acquaintances, and strangers. I posted generic messages on my timeline, as it was impossible to reply to everyone personally.

It didn't stop at virtual support: a friend started a crowd-funding scheme to help me with the costs. I was, and still am, immensely grateful for all those people who decided to help. Joining forces, they took a big weight off my shoulders and gave me space to grieve.

As soon as the press reported that Julian was dying, I started receiving, in addition to all the good wishes, messages that made my stomach turn. Thirty-six in all. Messages that spoke of 'justice'. About 'God and His punishment' for being gay. I found it reassuring that none of those messages came from a recognisable email address. Because, of course, they were sent anonymously. Cowardice is part and parcel of hate mail. So are grammatical errors.

Threatening letters were not new to us. We initially started receiving them after the first edition of *Et Alors?* They were full of shame, slander, and hatred, and threats like 'I know where you live.' It made me feel sick at first, but Julian never wanted to dwell on them. In her opinion, paying it even the smallest amount of attention would detract from all the positive work we did.

'There is only one thing in the world worse than being talked about, and that is not being talked about,' said Oscar Wilde. And, we realised that our work would always court controversy.

When our plan to marry twenty-two times first appeared in the press, the comments and letters became more vicious. They mentioned 'hanging' and said that we should be put against a wall and shot. The so-called 'promotion of homo-sexuality' apparently deserved torture techniques that would have made de Sade faint. Julian decided not to read any more comments. Neither the positive ones, nor the negative. She asked me to do the same. Because, after reading a hundred happy messages, it was human nature to only remember the one that said you should be dissolved in hydrochloric acid. Slowly.

Julian felt that this kind of negativity was making us reactionary. And our project was anything but that. On the contrary. If we enacted our performance from an anti-homophobia angle, it would only increase the energy from the opposite pole. If, on the other hand, we worked from an independent position, from detachment, then the project would take on a life of its own. Love is almost subversive in these times.

I thought of all her beautiful and enthusiastic words, as I read an email in which someone wished her to die a slow and painful death. I had to tell myself it wasn't personal. Not addressed to my wife, who was burning up with a fever lying next to me in bed.

=

Even now, after her death, the future is gradually moulding itself into a new shape and silently taking me with it. I say yes to everything, because every future prospect is a step forward. At a New York art opening, a handsome Asian man walks up to me and asks if I am Fleur Pierets. Taken by surprise, I nod. He introduces himself as a publisher and says he recognises me from a picture in *The Huffington Post*. And that he'd been wanting to contact me about a project for a while now. Charles is working on a series about diversity, for children aged between four and six years old. He asks me if I would be interested in writing a book about same-sex marriage. A children's book about two women, Fleur and Julian, who marry everywhere in the world where they are allowed. In the days that follow, we hash out all the details. In the book, Julian will not die after the fourth marriage, but instead we will finish the entire project. An illustrator will create the illustrations based on our photos, and I will write my perfect ending: after the last marriage, we will live happily ever after. Am I hoping to find my way back to the right reality this way, or am I madly deluding myself? Whatever the case is, I am once more able to add an extra three months to my timeline.

Whether you are gay, straight, bi,
whatever that is, we all love, we all hurt,
we all get angry and feel pain.

In conversation with Kanithea Powell
Et Alors? Magazine

THE DAY THEY CAME TO INSTALL THE BED AT MY MOTHER'S house, we could finally leave the hospital. Taking her home came with some strict rules. There was that bed, but also endless paperwork for the village doctor, who would check her pain medication every three days. And, she needed two nurses. One to bathe her and care for her, another to give her a daily injection to prevent phlebitis. I dismissed the first. Even at the hospital I had done everything myself, because no one could possibly be more careful with her than I was. Watching and wondering if they weren't hurting her made me very nervous. Since, by now she had become unable to move her arms and legs, I had become overprotective. I was okay with the nursing staff, as they could see that I was managing well. Every morning at six, a metal breakfast trolley was noisily wheeled into the room. Every morning I said it was not necessary. Because, my mother had brought fruit the day before so we wouldn't have to eat the unpalatable hospital food. A few minutes before six I gently woke Julian, to avoid having the trolley startle her. I made fruit salad, brewed tea, and sat down next to the bed to very slowly feed her bits of banana and orange. While doing this I told her about what I had supposedly dreamed of that night. She talked less and less, and she spoke very softly, as if she no longer had the strength to make a sound. When I asked her something, she usually couldn't find the answer, or she forgot what she wanted to say while she was trying to form a sentence. Sometimes, I would inquire what she had dreamed about, or ask her something different. Then, she would just look at me. I wanted to know where she thought she was going. Whether she was scared. What she wanted to happen after her death. But, those were all questions. So, I stopped asking them. I was left to guess what she felt, knew, understood, and saw.

I learned not to ask any more questions. I also learned to recognise her different phases. There was the phase where she looked at me and I saw she could see me. Often, she'd then say something, so we could still have a short conversation every now and then. Afterwards, she usually fell asleep very quickly. In another phase, she was conscious but unable to speak. This made her very sad. I'd try to talk to her without asking any questions, as I could see how much it frustrated her not to be able to answer. Yet another condition was when she was not 'clear' as I had started calling it, but she was able to speak. Those were the moments I had to brace myself against, because she sometimes said something hurtful. Since her memory was failing her, she sometimes got angry with me for being the one who fed her yucky pills, and bothered her with soap and water after breakfast. On a few occasions she was angry with me, because she had forgotten the diagnosis and thought I didn't want to make her better. 'You don't love me,' she'd say. I knew I shouldn't take it personally. But, the idea of her ever thinking that I didn't want the best for her still echoes in my nightmares.

There were times when all her memories were gone, but she was still aware of her situation and place. And, then there was the phase where she didn't know who or where she was at all. Fortunately, I was the one she trusted and smiled at. Even though I'm not sure if she still knew who I was.

Talking to her became a minefield, as within the space of an hour she could go through all these different states of consciousness. Sometimes I could recognise them by the darkening of her eyes, other times it was not visible at all. Some phases were very difficult to distinguish, because her facial expression didn't change. The only way for me to find out was – ironically – by asking her questions.

In the ambulance on the way to my mother's house I was very calm. It was a week since we'd left for the hospital and, unlike that outward journey, I was now allowed to sit next to her. Gazing at the fields and forests we drove by, I realised for the first time that without her the world would lose its colour. I became teary-eyed, but was jerked back to reality when she said, *don't cry*. I choked it all back and reassured her. When she fell asleep, the driver softly asked when she would be returning to the hospital. I said she wasn't going back: she was dying. Earlier, I had already put it in writing, but it was the first time that I'd said it outloud to a stranger. He kept looking straight ahead for the rest of the journey.

=

During my first lecture in New York, my hands are shaking and I realise once again how much strength and confidence Julian used to give me. I had always enjoyed talking about our work. We once spent two days at the Department of Defense talking about diversity, and a week talking about positive activism at a private boarding school. I have addressed classes of students aged from 12 to 22. Julian never spoke much, and let me do most of the talking. Still, I felt her presence and it made me strong.

I walk up the stairs to the stage, hoping that I won't drop to the floor or have to throw up.

When I catch sight of the three hundred people in the room, I knock over my microphone. 'That's a good start,' I say. And the audience laughs with me.

I'm amazed by the amount of passion in my body. As soon as I speak the first sentence, I'm off. It's a quote by Delacroix, and it's the essence of the work that Julian and I have done: 'What drives artists, what inspires their work is not the new ideas, but their obsession with the idea that what has already been said is not enough.' I talk about our world view and our research into identity. For an instant, my voice falters; it's when I suddenly wonder how long it will take before I automatically replace the word 'we' with 'I'. But, I pull myself together.

After I've talked for 40 minutes, the questions come. A lot are about our work, but after a while the first, albeit hesitantly, personal questions arise. The organiser looks at me and I let her know with a nod that it's okay. A girl asks if

I intend to continue working without Julian. I tell her I have no choice. That I still wake up every day with hundreds of ideas to create something that draws attention to human rights. Because, while in some places they have already been acquired, the acquired right nevertheless remains fragile, and should not be taken for granted. It can still be taken away just as quickly. But, I also tell her that I don't know how yet. That, of the two of us, Julian was the executive power, and that I often lack the technical knowledge or insight to know which medium is suitable for which work, but I do intend to find out, because I'm driven to do this work.

When someone else asks me, how do you know you love someone so much that you want to marry them twenty-two times, I feel myself becoming unsteady. Still, I force myself to answer and try to say, without sounding pathetic, that I knew it from the first moment I loved her more than life itself. The organiser ends the conversation when someone starts to sob and I bite my lip so hard that I can taste blood.

*We're shaped by our reality and
whether or not you're in transition,
you still should be moving onwards
with your work.*

In conversation with Rhyannon Styles
Et Alors? Magazine

THE HOSPITAL BED WAS IN THE ROOM NEXT TO THE LIVING
room, which formed a triangle with the kitchen. My mother
lit the fireplace every morning and I decorated the bedroom
with Christmas lights. Every now and then she painfully got
her foot stuck in the bedrail, so I had surrounded her with
pillows. It reminded me of a sick baby bird I found when I
was little, which I had nestled in a box of cotton balls.

It was shocking to witness how fast she was declining.
Since the diagnosis she had not had her period, she was
becoming more confused by the day and had begun making
strange statements. They seemed like fragments of conversations that she was turning into a new story for herself.
What story is she telling herself, I wondered? I hoped it was
beautiful, because mine was not.

Sometimes she was very realistic. Like, when she
asked me to thank the doctor every time he came by. She
did so herself, when she was lucid. Other days she spoke
in English. Once she asked how I was doing and if I had
a headache. Whether I was taking my medications. It

took me a while to realise that she thought I was the patient.

We were living in different realities, and that made us very lonely. Where, up until recently we'd been talking nonstop, it now seemed as if we no longer understood each other at all.

Her consciousness was disappearing more frequently, and I wondered where she went when she wasn't 'here.' And, whether it was a good place. What she dreamed of, and whether she was scared or sad. Her not being able to answer my questions made me feel powerless. She once said, out of nowhere, that she was afraid it would be 'dark and cold there.' I felt a panic attack coming on, yet I told her a story explaining why it couldn't be so. I don't remember what I said, it must have been nonsense, but I still remember my relief when she fell asleep in the middle of my litany.

=

In New York I fill my schedule with lectures, given by myself and others, with exhibitions and meeting up with friends. Some days are serene, but others I'm hyper-aware of every smell, every breath, and the texture of a sleeve against my bare arm. Times like these are exhausting, and I now recognise them as signals to go home. My breathing becomes shallow as I wait for a cup of takeaway soup and, panting, I climb the five flights of stairs to my rented room in Chelsea. I take off my clothes, change into a Metallica t-shirt and eat the soup standing in front of the window. I survey all the people walking at a rapid rate from one place to another, and I wish I had the energy to join them. Julian's absence surrounds me, and for the hundredth time I wish she were with me. She had settled into my body now, and was flowing through my bloodstream. I can feel her phantom-being seeking its way out of the interior walls of my skin. 'Why don't you just come back now,' I whisper softly to myself. 'You've been gone long enough now.'

I get under the covers with Wojnarowicz's *Closer to the Knives*: 'If I could attach our blood vessels so we could become each other I would. If I could attach our blood vessels in order to anchor you to the earth to this present time I would. If I could open up your body and slip inside your skin and look out your eyes and forever have my lips fused with yours I would.'

I think of the brave man who wrote this. Knowing he was dying, of the same disease he'd lost his partner to. I think of how symbiotic those two were, from the moment they met until Wojnarowicz took pictures of Hujar's lifeless body. Could it be that the dead are plagued by the wailing lamentations of their survivors? Am I hindering her in her progress, by trying so frenetically to bring her back to life?

According to Antonin Artaud, an artist is someone who walks a tightrope between visions and madness, someone undergoing an alchemical process, allowing himself to be melted down and transmuted, in order to recreate himself in his art. He could just as well have been talking about someone in mourning. I have good and bad days, but the madness always lingers beneath my skin. Sometimes, I feel strong and decisive for three days in a row. I try to cherish these days, because I quickly learn that a new crisis will arise every time.

Then, the hours and days drag on, but by now I know from experience that another moment will come when I will hesitantly allow myself to smile, wiggling my toes Uma Thurman-style, to pump new life into my body. After a crisis everything slows down, and showering and getting dressed takes more time. Like an elderly person, I hold on to the bannister as I walk down stairs, one at a time. Finally reaching the bottom, I open the front door, step outside, and close my eyes to fully take in the hum of cars and din of sirens. Time and again I decide to enjoy every second of relief as if I were feeling it for the first time. Until a conversation, a glance, or a smell brings me down again. But, that's for later.

For the moment, I am back. Still a bit shaky, but present.

It is reality we are willing to forget,
because we despise triviality.

In conversation with Leonoor Zwartevooghel
Et Alors? Magazine

WHEN JEROEN AND NIKKIE ARRIVED IN FRANCE, THEY brought some life with them. I had told them that Julian was having bad dreams about it being 'cold and dark' where she was bound to go. They hung a large dream catcher above her bed. Both my mother and I felt trapped in our grief, and it was good to be able to have a conversation with someone other than the village doctor; who every three days directed a helpless look at me while increasing her pain medication.

Inside, the fireplace was burning and my mother read books, while both Nikkie and Jeroen were writing their new novels at the dining table. Outside, it was snowing. Julian sometimes did and sometimes didn't respond to them, but most of the time she was calm at least. Once, she even laughed out loud seeing Jeroen, bundled up like a bear, towering over her bed after his morning walk.

The cosiness contrasted sharply with the pain I felt for my wife, who was disappearing so rapidly. The more her brain slipped, the more of her identity she lost. My sharp, funny, smart wife was gone, and she would have hated her own dependency.

I will always love you.
I will never forget you.
You are in my heart forever.
I will never leave you.

I looked at our domestic scene and remembered a comment she had made at the hospital: 'I won't leave until you're nicely settled in.'

Nikkie had cautiously asked me if I had already told Julian she could leave. She thought that was important, as my wife was someone who would hurt herself to spare me. I looked around and wondered if this was what she meant when she'd told me to be nicely settled in. The little lights above her bed were on, and I had lit candles all over the place.

The next time she woke for a moment, I gathered all my courage and whispered in her ear that the house was nice and cosy. And that she could leave if she felt she needed to.

Don't ever die, I had once told her, after her breast surgery. That time she had earnestly shaken her head. 'I won't die.' Now, I had to tell her she could leave, restraining myself from screaming hysterically, 'You promised!'

I sat next to her bed every day. Sometimes with my laptop. Often with a book. At night, I lay on a sofa in the same room. Even when she was asleep, I looked at her, taking her in with my eyes. I would never see her again. I touched her. I would never be able to touch her again. I gently brushed her arm, her hand, her face, with my lips. I'll never be able to do this again, I thought. My love for her was so complete and tangible that you could have scooped it up with a spoon.

During the day my mother, Nikkie, and Jeroen often came to sit with us. One of them would sometimes come and write at the table in her room, or sit on the other side of the bed and talk to me. Nikkie occasionally sang and played on her singing bowls; something Julian had always enjoyed and found soothing. I sought comfort in the fact that she smiled often. If she was smiling, it couldn't be all that bad. She might be pleased with the thoughts that were going through her head. I only left the room to take a shower in the morning. Then, my mother took my place next to the bed.

'Shouldn't you get outdoors for a while?' asked Jeroen, after I had spent another sleepless night. 'Your colour is like ...' he said. Nothing more. A writer lost for words, and I didn't even look in the mirror.

I'll have plenty of chances to go out, I thought. Later.

Their presence ensured that the atmosphere in the house was less depressing, and in the evening the four of us ate dinner at the table in Julian's room. At the foot of her bed. Sometimes she was asleep, often she was just resting. We talked softly among ourselves. About what I would do after her death. Jeroen was convinced that I should return to Antwerp for a while. At least for a little while, because I would need an emotional safety-net.

In retrospect, I don't think I could ever have guessed just how different anticipatory grief is from actual mourning. I could be angry with myself at times, for feeling so terribly lonely. After all, she was still there. How could I be lonely? But I missed her voice. For seven years we had been keeping each other informed of every thought. We had shared and discussed everything with each other. She used to sing improvised songs to me. Mostly with made-up rhyming words, but nevertheless so very sweet and charming. Now, she barely even uttered a sentence, with very long intervals in between. Sometimes those sentences were intelligible, but sometimes they were not. Her inability to understand, and having to admit it, was awful. But, then, all of a sudden she'd say something that proved she'd been paying close attention and, in a panic, I'd review everything I'd said earlier while she was sleeping, thinking she couldn't hear me. Guilt flooded my mind whenever I thought she might have heard me. That she'd heard me make a plan, no matter how trivial, that didn't include her. Maybe she thought I couldn't wait to be rid of her. Guilt killed any potential thoughts of improvement.

=

I never thought Julian would come back. Maybe that's the difference between sudden death and a six-week dying process. My book could be called *A Year in the Wrong Reality*. Although I'm well aware that this life is all there is for me, my mind begs to differ. Some days my thoughts are more science-fiction-like than others, but most of the time I feel like I was literally pushed into the wrong reality when Julian died. Other times, I think that every good thing that happened to me after her death is imaginary, and that in reality I am still lying under the covers in the dark. Musk's simulated reality still pops up all the time, and some days I look at my hands, thinking: this is not me.

The combination of consciousness and dream-state makes me immune to the fear of failure (it doesn't matter, as it probably isn't real anyway) and ensures that I have never looked at the world with such an open and non-judgmental mind. This unfiltered state brings people and possibilities with it that I would otherwise never have encountered.

When Andy Warhol was shot by Valerie Solanas, he said that thereafter he was never sure whether he'd really survived. Whether he had actually come back. He was almost certain that he was in dream-space, trapped in an intersection between two worlds. Warhol responded to this by withdrawing into himself even more. As for me, I'm turning my body inside-out, and I face the world more naked than ever.

I once told Julian that, as a teenager, I had read a book by actor and director Lee Strasberg, about his famous Actors Studio. I was fourteen, and attended a fine arts secondary school in Ghent. Rebellious, like any adolescent, but firmly convinced that I wanted to do great and, above all, fun things. Preferably abroad. As far away as possible from everything that I already knew. I read about the school that taught actors like Robert de Niro and Dustin Hoffman their acting techniques. Strasberg developed his method based on the Russian Stanislavski school and called the series of exercises he used for this *method acting*. A technique in which the actor falls back on their sensory memories from the past, in order to give form to the character or role. 'Acting isn't something you do,' Strasberg wrote in the book. 'Instead of doing it, it occurs.'

I told my wife that I had been very impressed by this. And that I'd wanted to take the bus to New York, and ask him to teach me everything he knew. From a young age I already had a talent for dramatic gestures.

'Why didn't you do that when you were older?'

'No idea. Things happen. Life happens, and you soon forget.'

A few weeks after our first trip to New York, and four years after this conversation, I woke up one morning and she said we were going on an adventure.

My clothes were lying on a chair in the bathroom, and she made tea while I got ready. During breakfast I questioned her, but she refused to say a word. I kept asking questions on the subway to Union Square, and while we were walking, until she stopped in front of a door. I raised my face and saw the banner with THE LEE STRASBERG THEATER AND FILM INSTITUTE. She had sent them a long email explaining that, as a fourteen-year-old, I had read the book and wanted to get on a bus there. But, she had also told them that she had been ill, that she'd had breast cancer, and that I had tirelessly cared for her.

A few days later she had received a message saying that they had read her mail with tears in their eyes. And that I was expected at the Marilyn Monroe Hall, to attend classes for three days. Something they otherwise never allowed.

I held her face in my hands and looked at her. 'Now who does something like that?' I asked. 'How can anyone be so incredibly nice?'

'You're pretty nice yourself,' she said. 'Off you go now, go act!'

Like an emotional masochist, I am now wandering through New York looking for all the places where I can conjure up these kinds of memories and adjust reality. I fantasise about what she would say to me (try to be nicer to yourself), I hear her laugh (what on earth are you doing?) and feel her hand on my arm (you're the best, you know?).

I believe all religions have beauty in
them whether or not god exists the way
we want him or her to exist. The only
thing I know is that we don't know
anything.

In conversation with Rolla Selbak
Et Alors? Magazine

THE ARRIVAL OF RENATE AND HER FRIEND MARC BROUGHT ME
a new realisation . Renate had always made me feel like
everything was going to be alright. This time, that was not
the case. I watched her closely as she entered our room, and
saw the shock on her face when she took in how Julian was
no longer Julian.

While I was talking with Renate about the meaning and
randomness of it all, Julian opened her eyes and said 'not
random,' and fell back to sleep. Was that a fraction of an
insight, or was she hearing and understanding everything
we were talking about? Did she see and know something we
couldn't possibly know? Somehow, one expects to hear the
gospel from someone who is near death.

Those moments when she opened her eyes, and I knew
that she really saw me, troubled me time and time again. She
saw me. Which meant that she was not completely gone, that
she still had a certain amount of consciousness. The thought
imposed itself: What if the doctors were wrong? Because she

just looked at me. Aware. What if she could still be cured? What if I'm harming her health by giving her all thes drugs?

Every day I moved the bar. Sometimes higher, sometimes lower, and sometimes vertically, depending on the thoughts that flashed through my mind. Because some glances were more lucid than the day before. Or, maybe they weren't, but the concept of lucidity acquired a different definition every day.

When, in the old days, we were watching a movie where someone was slowly deteriorating towards death, we often commented that the other person should just give them a shot. *But I mean it, you know*, she would say. And I promised. These are big words that can only be spoken in the light of love and immortality. When the time came, I chose to let nature or medicine take its course. By that point I had amassed enough morphine to knock out an elephant. But, I was selfish and wanted to keep her with me for as long as possible.

=

And then, there is the matter of faith. Only after Julian's death did I realise how much trust I had always placed in life. A deeply ingrained belief that everything would be fine, that I would always intuitively know which path to take, and that life had only good intentions for me. We had always been thankful. For each other, for my mother, for our possibilities. And, also, for our happiness. Several times a day even. We took nothing for granted, certainly not each other.

'Do you know how happy I am with you?' I often said.

'No, tell me.'

Every form of spirituality died with her. It's something I struggle very hard with. My search for helpful hints also includes a 'something' that makes it all worthwhile.

I've always called myself an agnostic. Not an atheist, because to say that God does not exist would be as dogmatic as to say that He does. For the sake of convenience, I call it 'trust,' but whatever it was, I've lost it, and besides the loss of Julian and the loneliness, it turns out to be one of my toughest hurdles.

The loss of faith, or the search for meaning, comes with an insane version of me. I try to keep her at a distance, but she is breathing so close to me that I can feel the hairs on the back of my neck stand up. Do crazy people know when they're going crazy? I wonder this as I look madness straight in the eye. She hasn't been around very long, that insane version of me. She appeared when someone said to me recently that God only gives you as much as you can handle. My insane Self reared up in front of me as those words sunk in. God gives you as much as you can handle. It makes me feel destructive, furious, demanding of answers. Ever since that crazy woman has been lurking, I've had to guard myself, and often at night I sit with my arms around my knees to stop myself from walking out the door, and taking the subway to the Bronx at 2 a.m. Or towards Central Park. In the dark. To find out what else 'Life' has in store for me. Because, then it had better happen all of a sudden. I imagine standing in the middle of the park. Free from fear. 'Do your worst!' I scream. Because, if life means well for me, then nothing will happen. So, I challenge fate. And I challenge destiny. I demand answers, and ask for proof that everything happens for a reason. That everything is not random and it's not all pure coincidence that the tumour grew in her head and not someone else's. But, since I don't know if crazy people know they're crazy, but I do know what impending madness feels like, I hold on to myself. With my arms around my knees. To keep myself indoors because, since she's gone, I no longer fear death. And that, along with a lack of trust, is the most destructive combination I can imagine.

Fearless people inspire me the most.
People who have the courage to aim for
their dreams and search for their goals.
For the things that make them truly
happy.

Editorial Issue 14
Et Alors? Magazine

THE SAME DAY, ONE YEAR LATER. EVERYONE HAD ALREADY gone to bed. I hoped they'd be raising a glass to their own health and happiness in their rooms. Julian was asleep, and I sat next to her bed and watched over her. I'd tried to tell her a few hours earlier that it was the last day of the year, but she hadn't understood what I was saying.

When the clock struck midnight, I realised that this was the year when I would lose my wife. The year I would be widowed. I opened my mouth and I screamed. Long, and without making a sound. Outside, there were fireworks.

=

Huffington Post editor Noah Michelson, whose body is 85 percent covered in tattoos, once said in an interview, 'Getting tattooed has allowed me to take the things that I could never get off my chest and literally put them on my chest. It's a kind of celebration, a form of bloodletting and a chance to capture the ephemeral and release it into my skin where it can mourn or sing or scream — sometimes all three at once — for the rest of my life.'

When someone asks me if I don't mind having those drawings on me forever, I shrug. Time has become a peculiar concept over the past year. I could get run over by a bus tomorrow, or get cancer, so chances are that the drawing won't be on there for very long. I tell stories on my skin. Sometimes they are shapes, like the circle with the line through it on my back. Or the lines on the back of both my legs, running from my heels to my buttocks. Like the seams of nylon stockings. And the double horizontal lines on my wrist, the equal sign, representing equality and the logo of the Human Rights Campaign.

Sometimes they are words, such as the Tennessee Williams quote, 'A prayer for the wild of heart that are kept in cages,' from his 1941 play, *Stairs to the Roof*.

In New York, I decide that I need to add another one. The word I associated with my stay: 'unapologetic.' It's a word that weaves itself through everything I see and hear. From Wojnarowicz's work to Cave's music.

I attend a lecture by Charlene A. Carruthers, a queer, feminist writer and champion for racial equality. The title of her book turns out to be *Unapologetic*. It's a word that makes me reflect on the work that I have done, and that I still want to do. About this book, where I will write what I need to write.

The tattoo artist nods in approval when I tell him what I want, and how the word should follow a line running diagonally from the inside of my wrist, up towards my armpit, and then wrap around my arm. 'It suits you,' he says. It takes a long time and is painful. Meanwhile, he asks me about my life, my stay in New York. The pain makes me disregard my innate reserve, and I tell him everything. He nods, asks more questions and continues. When he's done, he ties cling film around my arm. He looks at me, briefly strokes my cheek and says: 'Now, you go and be fearless. You can do this.' Possessed by a newfound vigour I have never felt before, I step out and onto Broadway. The endorphin rush from all the pain makes me feel something that almost resembles happiness.

There isn't really much of a gap between my reality and my art. I've let it envelop me and I don't think I would ever change that.

In conversation with Joe Black
Et Alors? Magazine

WHEN I RAN OUT OF WORDS, I READ TO HER. I HAD ABANDONED Murakami when I noticed his surrealism was clouding her dreams. I remembered a wonderful book by Toon Tellegen: *Maybe They Knew Everything*. A collection of short stories about forest animals. About the squirrel and the ant. About their friendship. And their adventures in which they eat a lot of cake. Together with an elephant. For his birthday.

Miraculously, the Dutch e-book was for sale on my Spanish Kindle, and I could see from her shining eyes that she liked the stories.

'Don't read too fast,' she said one day. 'Otherwise the book will end.'

I swallowed my tears. She would never make it to the end of the book. No matter how fast I read.

I measured her life by the number of stories she would get to hear. I read them all beforehand, while she was sleeping. So I could select the most beautiful ones. I marked the sad stories with a black flag. I skipped those.

How trapped must she have felt when her language fell away? In an attempt to stem the aching flow of pity, I sometimes told myself she was unaware of it. But I still remember exactly how she looked at me and how I tried with all my might to comprehend her truncated words and sentences that usually didn't make any sense to me. I was, however, the only one of our housemates who could still understand anything. Whenever she said something, Jeroen, Nikkie, Renate, Marc and my mother all looked at me, and now and then I was able to translate. I tried so hard, and I noticed her frustration when I failed.

I read to her until she fell asleep. About the squirrel who feels a need to learn to count and asks a sparrow to teach him. After a month, he can count to seven, but the ant is not impressed. 'What's a seven?' she asks.

My muscles were cramping. I was holding my e-reader in one hand. I sat on the edge of the bed, where there was not nearly enough space, with my other arm around her. Hovered above her, as I couldn't rest the full weight of my arm on her. When she fell asleep, I tried to gently stretch my back. My throat was hoarse and dry. I put my hand in her hand and she opened her eyes. Before, she had caramel-coloured eyes, with specks of gold. Since a few days ago they had become completely black. She looked at me with those dark eyes and I noticed she saw me. Really saw me.

'You are the best squirrel there is,' she said. And she fell back to sleep. It was the last thing she would ever say.

=

'How do you paint death? How do you paint loss? How do you paint guilt in a way that isn't sentimental? In a terrible way, George's death gave Bacon the great subject of his painting. It was about loss, about grief, about guilt, because he felt guilty that he hadn't managed to save George from killing himself.' This is what Michael Peppiatt, friend and biographer of the painter Francis Bacon wrote.

The relationship between Bacon and George Dyer was turbulent from the start. Bacon, fascinated by criminals and the danger that they entailed, met Dyer in 1963. By that time, Dyer had already spent more time inside than outside prison. With Bacon he found his purpose in life, as the artist's companion and muse. Bacon took Dyer away from the criminal lifestyle by giving him enough money so he wouldn't have to steal, and placed him into the over-sophisticated art world. Their relationship was dysfunctional from the start, and marked by alcoholism, passion, and violence. Still, Dyer would, in life as in death, have the greatest influence on Bacon's work.

By 1971, Dyer had attempted suicide several times. Bacon had always found him in time to have his stomach pumped at the hospital. On 24 October, two days before Bacon's triumphant retrospective at the Grand Palais in Paris, Dyer succeeded. He overdosed on alcohol and sleeping pills in their hotel bathroom. Bacon went through with the exhibition, but said years later: 'If I had stayed with him at the time and not been busy with the preparations, he would still be here. But I didn't, and now he's dead.'

How do you paint death? How do you paint loss? How do you paint guilt? What followed were four years of uninterrupted work in which the artist tried to tame his demons. In retrospect, they turned out to be the strongest works in his entire oeuvre.

=

New York brings new friendships. I find one of them at a party where I'm scrutinising someone wearing sunglasses and wondering where I know him from.

'Bono. U2,' someone informs me.

"Course!' I say. And I turn to Stefan Andemicael, a man with dreadlocks down to his knees.

That night we became friends, and in the weeks that follow we have conversations late into the night. At seedy dive bars in the East Village, where the girls behind the bar wear Debby Harry shirts and try out their cocktail experiments on us. With alcohol for Stefan, mine without. He books artists for Blue Note, and takes me to exclusive clubs where we carry on, yelling into each other's ears over the loud music. Noticing how we have a calming influence on each other, we decide to meet at a coffee bar and work together. No words, but his proximity soothes me. In one of those working moments a hummingbird flies in. A hummingbird in New York. The tiny creature circles around a few times, and then flies out the door again.

'The hummingbird is a symbol of resilience and adaptability. It guides us back to our past, showing us that we must not dwell on it and that we need to move joyfully forward,'

Stefan reads aloud after looking up the bird's symbolism.

'What a coincidence,' I say.

'Or an instruction manual,' he says.

In the first few months after her death, obsessed with other women's experiences, I often read about how their environment forced them to go on living. Before long, they were faced with platitudes like, 'You're still young' and 'Aren't you over it yet?' My friends aren't doing that. They give me space to grieve, and are there when I need them. Stefan becomes one of them. He's taking me to Coney Island, because I had once mentioned that I loved multicoloured lights and anything that sparkles. Like a magpie. He's unaware of my history with that glittering place. With the Ferris wheel, the Boardwalk boulevards, and the scent of the sea mingling with pink candyfloss. With the night we spent there a year ago, in all that strange, beautiful company. I'm a romantic, even now, and the lights and clatter of the roller coaster still have the same exhilarating, yet calming, effect on me. I wonder what it must feel like to live here, to be a part of this little patch of land so filled with noise. So dazzlingly bright, and where people only come for the distraction, the excitement, and the amazement.

'Look. It's you!' Julian said at the time, pointing to a little wooden mermaid with red hair and blue eyes.

'Look. It's you!' says Stefan, pointing at the statue. I have to suppress the urge to put my head on his shoulder and ask him to tell me that everything will be okay. Instead, I close my eyes for a moment, swallow my tears, and listen to the screams of the people on the roller coaster, the sizzle of churros in oil, and the absence of her voice that whispered 'I am so very happy with you' in my ear, at that same spot, just one year ago.

THE MORE HER ILLNESS PROGRESSED, THE LESS NOISE SHE could tolerate. A loud footstep made her flinch. When she was awake, she was in pain, and she woke up at the slightest thing. Jeroen, Nikkie, Renate, and Marc were having a hard time, as they had to tiptoe and whisper their way through the house. After five weeks I asked them to leave. For their own sake, for mine, but especially for Julian. I felt that she needed the rest, and that she would not live much longer now.

Nobody was thrilled by the idea of leaving us by ourselves. For days, Renate had been urging me to try and sleep at night. Something I refused to do, as it would force me to rediscover reality every morning. Nikkie often found me crying on the living-room floor, in the middle of the night, when I had left the bedroom for a moment so as not to wake Julian. All of us were helplessly watching the staggering calamity in progress.

=

I still expect to be surprised, and every day I hope to hear, see or feel Julian's presence. However, reality is relentless and cold, and from the lack of her presence I'm now looking for any signs I can hold on to. I'm still reading continuously. Several books a week, sometimes up to four at a time. Once I get into something I will not let go. I won't stop searching until I find a satisfying and logical answer. What used to be a strength is now turning into a useless obsession, and I feel I will never understand why this is happening. My life is going round in circles. In one of those circles, I keep encountering Nick Cave and I tell Stefan that it looks like he is my spirit animal.

When Julian died, a friend gave me the documentary *One more time with feeling*. Cave lost his fifteen-year-old son Arthur, who fell from a 66 foot-high cliff in Brighton. Not wanting to talk to journalists, Cave made a documentary about the creation of his new album. A camera crew followed the band during the recording of *The Skeleton Tree*. It is the record of a grieving process. Cave poured his pain into a mould and the mould fits me. I still drag the music with me all over the place. In bed, in the bath, on the plane, and on my aimless walks through the city, where I occasionally place my hand against a building to check if the world around me is still real.

When asked by a fan if he and Susie still felt Arthur's presence, Cave replied, 'I feel the presence of my son, all around, but he may not be there. I hear him talk to me, parent me, guide me, though he may not be there. Dread grief trails bright phantoms in its wake. These spirits are ideas, essentially. They are our stunned imaginations re-awakening after the calamity. Like ideas, these spirits speak of possibility. Follow your ideas, because on the other side of the idea is change and growth and redemption. Create your spirits. Call to them. Will them alive.'

I'm jealous. Jealous because I want to feel that presence too. I could live with the idea that it's an illusion. That wouldn't matter to me. As long as she is here, in whatever form. I have to take her with me in everything I do. My lack of faith and spirituality is working against me, but Cave's 'Will them alive' resonates. I dream up one photo series after another, and already there's a number of projects in the works. As if I can make her live on through art. Perhaps it's only a small step in willing her alive, through writing and photomontages. Even if it's just to prevent myself from going insane. The world is too empty without her, and I know this is a pivotal point in my thinking. I need to go in search of beauty in order to defeat reality. I am a half, and no one will take her place. I will have to become whole from within myself.

I seek my consolation in art and in words. 'Beauty is a balm for grief,' wrote Bill Hayes after his husband Oliver Sacks died. I understand very well what he is saying, because everything I find beautiful continues to play on my mind for days, sometimes weeks. There is no substitute for love, no substitute for touching and kissing, but slowly my own images are forming a clear pattern in my head. Whether I'd still have anything to say without Julian has turned out to be an unfounded fear. The opposite is the case, and I fill notebook after notebook, the black-and-white Staples type, with ideas, drawings, plans, and statistics.

When I hear that Nick Cave is performing in New York I try seeing it as a sign. Witnessing a live performance of my mourning album makes past and present collide. At the concert I let my hair fall down in front of my face because I don't want the bystanders to see my tears. There are eight months between the first time I heard the album and the moment I hear him sing the songs live. How much and how little has happened in that time. I have felt alive a few times already. Have already laughed, and even had some nice days and evenings. The despondency and sadness remain, but I'm amazed at how strong my urge for optimism is. I am still aware that I gave myself two years. A little more than a year to go. If I still feel as much grief as I do now, then I can leave. The thought continues to comfort me. The subway from the concert hall back to Manhattan is overcrowded, and for the first time, more than half of the people don't pull out their phones. Most of them are looking straight ahead, still under the spell of the music. Almost everyone is softly humming the song we left the concert with.

I got a feeling I just can't shake
I got a feeling that just won't go away
You've gotta just keep on pushing, keep on pushing
Push the sky away.

Later on I will have a chance to talk to him, during his Conversations with Nick Cave. I tell him that since he said

'Will them alive,' I have worked so hard to feel her next to me again, but I can't. 'So, how?' I ask. And I'm embarrassed by the tears in my voice. 'Pretend,' he says, looking straight at me. 'It doesn't matter that it's not real. Pretend. Until you believe it. It's the only way you can survive.'

*This is what I'm supposed to do. It's as
simple as that. It's just who I am and I
know that if I would stop, I would be
very unhappy.*

In conversation with With Le Pustra
Et Alors? Magazine

IT HURT TERRIBLY TO SEE JEROEN, NIKKIE, RENATE, AND MARC
leave, but I knew it was for the best. I knew I shouldn't have
any distractions around me in those last days. I only left the
room to use the toilet and drank as little water as possible
so as not to have to do that very often. Julian had stopped
eating some days earlier, and I followed suit. I read to her,
touched her, and sang songs in a whisper: 'The Way You
Look Tonight.' 'Fly Me to the Moon.' Every now and then I
saw a twinkle in her eye. Probably because I can't sing at all.

> *Some day, when I'm awfully low,*
> *When the world is cold,*
> *I will feel a glow just thinking of you*
> *And the way you look tonight.*

Sometimes I was amazed at the big smile I felt creeping
across my face. Like when I was brushing her teeth and she
didn't remember what to do with the water in her mouth.
Then, I held out a cup and made a little spitting sound. She

followed my lead and smiled. There was so much love in the room. It grew much larger than me and I wrapped it around her, beamed it at her, and intuitively felt that she knew. That nothing else existed but the two of us. I didn't feel love as much as became love, and my tears were of profound unity. Finally, words were no longer needed.

=

Last night I dreamed of Julian for the first time. After more than nine months. There were many versions of her. All wearing suits. And many versions of me. All in a light blue angora sweater. We found our real 'me' among all the replicas and she took my face in her hands: 'I love you.' I wake up crying so hard that I worry I'll wake my housemates up. I lie on my back in bed, staring at the flaking ceiling until dawn. I take a shower and join the morning crowd on 9th Avenue. Their haste, their coffee cups, still have a calming effect on me. It's late October and New York is getting colder.

I step into the heartbeat of the city and let it synchronise with mine. Sometimes a bit faster, sometimes a bit slower, depending upon the memories I encounter along the way.

The dream has flustered me, and I walk from my room to Central Park for an hour. I forgot my notebook and ask the hot dog vendor for some napkins. Like a maniac, I fill them with scribbles while watching the squirrels run in and out of the trees. I only notice how cold I am when it starts to rain harder. I throw my napkins in the trash and walk past people in crazy costumes. It's Halloween and in my favourite book-store they're playing Tim Burton soundtracks and the staff are all wearing animal noses. I wish they'd all worn a fake nose, like Nicole Kidman's when she played Virginia Woolf in *The Hours*. It would be a neat reference for a bookstore.

I would have loved to tell you this, I think.

On the street I'm disconcerted by the idea that I can no longer tell the difference between the madmen and those who have put on a costume. I should have bought a mask.

For weeks now I have been making up different theories about the meaning of life and Stefan is a willing ear.

'If you could be anything you wanted to be, are you on the right track now?' I ask him.

My condition is one of endless possibilities and within the parameters that I have to do it without Julian, anything is possible, because I literally have nothing left to lose. It's my point zero. And, if I can choose who I want to be and what I want to do, am I moving in the right direction? As I ask him that question, I realise that I must be careful not to plunge my friends into an existential crisis. A few days later I share my final conclusion.

'Either life is totally random or we are in the wrong reality. It's one of the two.' Stefan joins me on my emotional rollercoaster, and sometimes laughs in my face. I can take it from him. Julian would have liked him a lot. He sees every emotion for what it is. Whether it's anger, euphoria, or irritation, he assigns them all equal value and, in that way, attempts to separate fiction from facts. I hope this fine trait is contagious because, so far, I can only rage until I collapse exhausted, and have a new theory every week. About what has actually happened, and what is going on. He listens to my babbling and joins me in my quest for magic. Sometimes I think he is secretly laughing at me. Like the time when he asked me what I wanted from life and I showed him the movie *Fur* with Nicole Kidman. 'That's how I want to live, I declared theatrically. He was kind enough not to point out that Diane Arbus committed suicide at the age of forty-eight.

To Stefan I confess my fear that this reality will never again be sufficient, and that I'm desperate to find out what else life holds in store. Because it's got to be impossible that this is all there is, that there is nothing more than this: great love, happiness, death, then nothing.

'I want to live and feel all the shades, tones and variations of mental and physical experience possible in my life. And I am horribly limited.' Sylvia Plath. I feel what she's saying. My limitation is that I have seen too much to be able to look at everything around me in amazement.

When I tell him that, perhaps I'll need to do some drugs, to see more beauty, he intervenes by making me promise to never try it with anyone but him. New York is in a mind-altering place and at every party you are offered LSD or pills. I promise, and he says maybe I should start with weed. Previous experiences, when my mother suddenly decided to 'go for the joints' and Jeroen and I happily went in with her, had usually ended with my head over the toilet bowl. The climax was my hallucination of a naked Norman Mailer in my room.

Rigid with tension, and the expectation of what might happen, I smoke half a joint, but all that happens is that my short-term memory no longer functions properly: by the end of a sentence, I no longer know how I started it. Unfortunately,

I do remember everything that has happened in recent months.

There is no difference between my state of being as a human, an artist, ascetic, aesthete or devotee of beauty. I simply seek to be. 'Kun', meaning 'to be', is a mystic Islamic state of being.

In conversation with Tareq De Montfort
Et Alors? Magazine

AS SOON AS HER BREATHING STARTED TO FALTER, I INTUITIVELY knew that she only had a few more hours to live. She was lying on her side and I had aligned my body with hers. My hand on her hand, my face against her neck. I could feel the heat of her fever.

I will always love you.
I will never forget you.
You are in my heart forever.
I will never leave you.

Never before had I felt so much love, and I did not know where she ended and I began.

Now and then I felt myself drifting off, and then jerked back to consciousness as the pauses between her breaths lengthen. I forced myself to stay awake and had to struggle against my mind and body's attempts to shield themselves from what was happening. Outside, the day was dawning and I was furious at the sun for shining so effortlessly while my worst nightmare was coming true.

Then the moment came when I knew she would breathe just three more times, just twice, just once.

=

I have breakfast with raspberry pie in my favourite coffee bar. In an ideal world, my wonderful wife would have turned forty-one today. I lean my chin on my hand and watch the people around me. A surly teenage girl sits next to me on the red velvet sofa. She reads Titus Andronicus and her mouth moves along with the words on the paper.

One of the characters in Chimamanda Ngozi Adichie's *Half of a Yellow Sun* says, 'When X died, it seemed like I was born again. I was a new person because I no longer had someone to remind me of what I had been.' I slowly discover a new me that is no better or worse than the one before. I did become stronger, though. But, that was not necessary. Even with Julian I was strong enough. I have lost many of my ideals, but I also notice that new ones are emerging. Not better, not worse. I have not yet regained my faith in life, but it did me good to read a book in which Stephen Hawking proves, based on the laws of physics, that God does not exist.

I hear that the grieving process gets worse in the second year, and I can't imagine anything that can exceed my grief of the past year in terms of 'badness.' The realisation that she is no longer there becomes clearer every day. The fog lifts, leaving me in an icy truth. Looking back at everything that has happened I realise that time does not heal all wounds. At best, it makes my shield a little less fragile. The possibility exists that it could still get worse.

This story has no happy ending and no closure. According to director David Lynch, that isn't necessary either. He calls the closing of a story a form of death.

I have chosen to live on, for now. And to continue working. Over the past year, I've learned that life goes on, but that I would still trade everything I have for one day with her. That I know what the term love pain feels like. That I keep looking for her in the faces of others, and that I still love her more than I love life. I've learned that grief is larger than myself, and that it is useless to try to exorcise it with logic and decisiveness. That the need to know why this has happened will never disappear, but that I'd better learn to bow my head to all the things I can't explain.

Nietzsche once wrote, 'What doesn't kill you makes you stronger.' I've always considered that a romantic idea, but today I dismiss it as a hollow cliché. What happened may not kill me, but it has cut me to the quick. It has ripped my heart out and left me breathless. What doesn't kill you makes you different. Or weirder. But, I'll do my very best to learn how to live with it.

I learn to overcome my relentless uncertainty as I wonder where she is now. Because, I don't know how she is doing. Because I hope it's not dark and cold out there. I learned that my mother and my friends were moving around me like tightrope walkers for months, but now they are providing the firm ground beneath my feet. From them I have learned that there is love even in the darkest times.

I still don't feel her presence. Not when I go to sleep and not when I wake up alone. Not when I want to talk to her, not when I want to put my hand on her cheek and tell her that I love her. Not when I want to tell her how lonely I am without her. But I know that she lives on in me and in the work that I do. I'll have to settle for this. But I still have to learn how.

So much love and thanks to my hardcore emotional safety net: Ingrid Van den Bossche, Renate Breuer, Rachida Aoulad, Peter Platel & Luc Acke.

My Dutch publisher Das Mag.

Thank you Bibiana Mas for the trust.

FLEUR PIERETS IS AN AWARD-WINNING BELGIAN PERFORMANCE artist, writer, speaker and LGBTQ+ activist whose work balances photography and theory, performance and non-fiction. Together with her wife Julian P. Boom, she founded *Et Alors?*, a magazine featuring conversations with queer musicians, visual artists, writers and performers. In 2017, Fleur and Julian launched *Project 22*, a performance art piece in which the couple planned to get married in every country that had legalised same-sex marriage at the time. Following the untimely death of her wife in 2018, after only four marriages, Fleur turned to writing, which led to her debut memoir in English, *Julian* (3TimesRebel Press, 2023).

Pieret's two-volume children's book, *Love Around the World* and *Love is Love*, in which Fleur and Julian fulfil the beautiful dream of Project 22, was published in the USA by Six Foot Press in 2020. A children's book (October 2023) and a novel (autumn 2024) are forthcoming from Dutch publisher Das Mag. Pierets is a regular speaker on LGBTQ+ issues at companies and institutions around the world, including Google and the UN.

ELISABETH KHAN IS A BELGIAN-BORN WRITER, EDITOR AND translator based in Ann Arbor, Michigan. From 2006 to 2013, she was editor-in-chief of the bilingual publication 'Gazette van Detroit.' Her short stories and poetry have appeared in various American literary magazines. She has translated several works of fiction and non-fiction from Dutch into English and from English into Dutch.

annapont

We translate female authors who write in minority languages. Only women. Only minority languages. This is our choice.

We know that we only win if we all win, that's why we are proud to be fair trade publishers. And we are committed to supporting organisations that help women to live freely and with dignity.

We are 3TimesRebel.